M|NDVESTOR

SERGE EL DFOUNI

PASSIONPRENEUR®
PUBLISHING

MINDVESTOR

The Definitive Guide to
Mastering Investments for Success

SERGE EL DFOUNI

PASSIONPRENEUR®
PUBLISHING

Publishing information
Publishing and design facilitated by Passionpreneur Publishing
A division of Passionpreneur Organization Pty Ltd
ABN: 48640637529

Melbourne, VIC | Australia
www.passionpreneurpublishing.com

To all the dreamers who dare to take a chance, to the beginners seeking knowledge and guidance, to the seasoned investors striving for growth, and to the pro investors constantly pushing boundaries— this book is dedicated to you.

To those who have supported this journey—whether through encouragement, mentorship, or simply by believing in my vision—your faith has been the fuel that propels me forward. This dedication is a tribute to your unwavering support and belief in the pursuit of financial freedom and abundance.

To the friends and family—especially my mom—who have stood by me, offering support and encouragement as I embarked on this journey of growth and wealth-building.

Here's to a future where financial literacy empowers individuals to shape their own destinies, where investing becomes not just a means to wealth accumulation but a path to personal fulfillment and societal impact. May this book serve as a beacon of knowledge and insight on your journey towards financial independence and prosperity.

A special thanks to my wife, who has supported me the most each step of the way, kept me pushing forward, and encouraged me when I needed it the most. I dedicate these pages to you. Your belief in me was my fuel when doubts crept in and I wanted to give up.

Cheers to new beginnings, bold decisions, and a life transformed by the magic of investing with purpose and passion.

CONTENTS

Acknowledgements...ix

Introduction...xi

Chapter 1
GETTING UNSTUCK 1

Chapter 2
THE EVOLUTION OF FINANCIAL MARKETS.............. 11

Chapter 3
BUILDING A WEALTH MINDSET................................ 29

Chapter 4
MASTERING RISK AND REWARD................................ 53

Chapter 5
INVESTING IN YOURSELF AND YOUR FUTURE 69

Chapter 6
PASSIVE VERSUS ACTIVE INVESTING........................ 79

Chapter 7
UNLOCKING THE POTENTIAL OF
REAL ESTATE INVESTMENTS 93

Chapter 8
NO ONE CAN PREDICT THE MARKET! 125

Chapter 9
CRYPTO, BLOCKCHAIN, NFTs ... WHAT'S GOING ON?!..... 133

Conclusion: Be Prepared for the Future 151
Works Cited 153
About the Author.. 155
Extras/Offer.. 157

ACKNOWLEDGEMENTS

I would like to express my heartfelt gratitude to all those who have contributed to the creation of this book. Your support, encouragement, and expertise have been invaluable throughout this journey.

First and foremost, I want to thank my family for their unwavering love and belief in me. Your constant encouragement kept me motivated during the challenging times of writing this book.

I am also grateful to my friends for their understanding and patience as I immersed myself in the writing process. Your words of encouragement and listening ears were sources of great comfort.

To my mentors and coaches, thank you for guiding me with wisdom and sharing your knowledge. Your insights have been instrumental in shaping this book into what it is today.

I extend my appreciation to all my business associates who have supported me along the way. Your collaboration and feedback have been invaluable in bringing this project to fruition.

A special thanks to the dedicated members of the publishing team who worked tirelessly behind the scenes to make this book a reality. Your expertise and professionalism have been truly remarkable.

Lastly, I want to thank all those who have believed in me and supported me on this journey. Your contributions, no matter how big or small, have made a significant impact on this book.

This book would not have been possible without each and every one of you. Thank you for being a part of this incredible journey.

INTRODUCTION

'TO BE A SUCCESSFUL BUSINESS OWNER AND
INVESTOR, YOU HAVE TO BE EMOTIONALLY
NEUTRAL TO WINNING AND LOSING.
IT IS ALL PART OF THE GAME.'

—ROBERT KIYOSAKI

Coming from where I come from, you wouldn't think that I would've ever made it as big as I have. In fact, the very fact that I've made it this far confuses many people! How could I, a random man from Beirut, make it to Dubai and successfully so?! I get it—it doesn't make sense, but it certainly makes for a *great* story, and one that I hope you'll be able to relate to!

See, I grew up in Lebanon. At the time, the country was experiencing conflict and war, both things that affect your chances of becoming 'someone' or doing something out of the ordinary from what's generally expected in Beirut. Lebanon, to this day, is still struggling to get past its current economic place in the world, with corruption having a tight grip on the country's finances and public spending. But back then, things were far worse! My family struggled to make ends meet, as one can imagine, and this became the *fuel* for me to look for a different path out of poverty. I remember sitting on the balcony one day and watching people walking down the street. There were a few stores down the opposite block—a pharmacy, a clothing shop, a ladies' salon … I'd people-watch whenever I felt down or depressed. I'd look at their behaviors and at how they were moving around. It would distract me from my reality—I felt hopeless and in despair after a series of disappointments. But this is when it all changes. For some reason, something clicked within me, a voice saying, 'What if you can change your reality? What if you have the power within you? What if you have control over your life?'

These questions opened my mind to new possibilities that led me to ask more questions like: 'How can I start? How can I seek help? What do I have to do today?' Something shifted inside me, and I had an idea. The next day, I went to a library and asked the manager, who was very nice and welcoming, to recommend a book with methods, tips, or strategies that could help change my reality. He smiled and told me that it was a tough request. After some thought, he suggested the book *Think and Grow Rich* by Napoleon Hill. I quickly bought the book and started reading.

I picked up practical principles and invaluable insights to empower myself to transform my mindset, set clear goals, cultivate supportive relationships, persist in the face of challenges, and harness the power of visualization for success. I took those learnings and put them into practice, taking action in the present moment, making choices and decisions that would lead me toward my desired future. I had to become and embody the person who could take me far in life.

I was sitting in the office on a different stormy winter day, looking outside through the window, watching rain fall from the sky and thinking, 'No one's going to help me. I have to help myself.' I felt cornered, with no escape plan. My parents were busy with their own struggles, my friends were living for the day, shortsighted, with no vision or dreams, and no serious talk. I had no connections, and I felt stuck. Yet something had changed within me. I realized that no one would care about my dreams but me, and the only way to break free was to take control. It hit me that ultimately, I was responsible for making changes, and it was in my hands to alter the course of my life and seek support from others who could provide valuable insights and resources.

I have the power. I came to the conclusion that change ultimately starts from within, and the key to initiating change lies within me, my mindset, and my determination. I had deep-rooted motivations and beliefs to change my circumstances, and I desperately wanted to succeed and build a future. This drive affected my behaviors, and I became laser-focused on the end result: my dream to become a successful businessman.

I gained confidence because I had clarity. I knew that my 'why' was to support my parents and provide them with the best that life could offer. I wanted to build a career for myself and become a businessman. This clear intention of knowing what I wanted started to help me develop a clear understanding of my goals, values, and purpose. It became easier to make decisions and take actions with conviction. Gaining clarity on what I wanted provided me with a sense of direction and purpose, allowing me to focus my energy on what truly mattered to me. With each step I took toward my goals, I experienced a boost in confidence as I became more aligned with my authentic self and the path I wanted to pursue.

So, I moved to Dubai. I had to change my reality. I had to do things *differently*. I just couldn't stay in Beirut any longer, only to end up stuck in Lebanon and never able to improve my circumstances! So, at the age of 26, I decided to move to Dubai. I had nothing, except for determination, ambition, and commitment. I was ready to build something for my family, my life, and my future—and thankfully, I did!

From that modest beginning, I embarked on a series of leaps and bounds. I transitioned from a small studio in Sharjah with a humble mattress to Deira, then to International City, and on to Discovery Gardens, finally settling in a 5-star hotel for five years. A few years ago, I moved to a beach house on Palm Jumeirah Island, surrounded by the sea and beautiful scenery. With each move, I aimed higher, craving a better lifestyle and pushing the boundaries of what was possible. Alongside my relentless pursuit of personal growth, I climbed the corporate ladder with dedication. Starting as a Warehouse Keeper, I moved on to roles like Data Entry, Logistics Officer, and Inventory Controller. Eventually, I reached positions such as Store Manager, Brand Manager, Channel Manager, and Vice President, always striving for excellence.

I think what really pushed me forward was my fear of ending up poor again. I was driven by a fear of scarcity, of being helpless and powerless with no money and no control over my future. I knew one thing for sure—I never wanted to be that guy ever again, so determination, commitment, and seriousness grew in me to a point where there was no coming back. Fear is normally what holds us back and prevents us from progressing in life—but in my case, fear was the fuel that kept me moving forward no matter what!

I used fear to progress in life and it was impossible to progress without change. 'Those who cannot change their minds cannot change anything' (as per George Bernard Shaw), so I decided right there that I needed to change and that *I* was the turning point for me.

I'm so thankful and grateful for the life I live today. When I look back and see how far I've come, from where I used to be to where I stand today, I feel happy and fulfilled. I'm living the life I always wanted, having the freedom to do whatever I want, whenever I want, with whom I want, and in the way I want. I'm living life on my own terms. Most importantly, I've been able to provide for and support my family, parents, and loved ones, and this alone is priceless!

I've traveled the world, explored different cultures and cities, driven luxury cars, made millions of dollars, owned real estate, built companies from the ground up, and become a shareholder and board member of a nine-figure global company. I've become the businessman I always aspired to be, achieving personal fulfillment and living beyond fear.

On a personal level, I'm no longer the person I used to be. I've grown to be more mature, wise, fulfilled, and grateful for everything I've accomplished, on both a personal and a professional level. I constantly strive to be the best version of myself, always aiming to be better than I was yesterday, setting new goals and pursuing them despite fear and doubts. As you grow, you encounter more problems and challenges, but it's all part of the journey, and I've learned to enjoy it along the way.

The illustration below explains it all. I've always had it engraved in my mind!

But none of this would have been possible if I'd had the wrong mindset. Had I allowed myself to stay in this

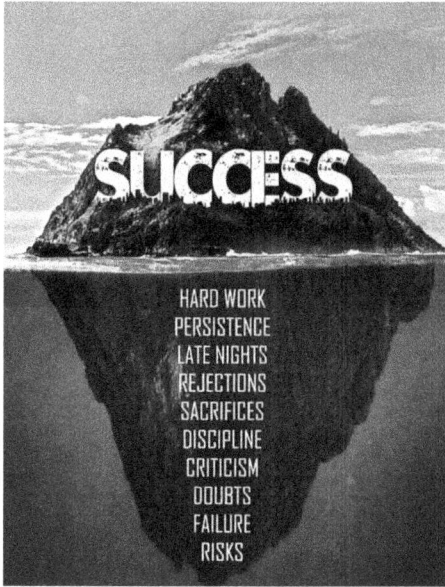

position, to continue being stuck in my country, I wouldn't have been able to achieve what I've achieved today. So, this book isn't only about teaching you all you need to know about finance—it's also about understanding that for it all to work well, you *need* to have the right mindset. You need to believe that you can achieve anything you want to achieve.

And look, money's something that most people never really understand throughout their lives. They might know a *little bit*, but while they're trying to make ends meet and manage to do so relatively well, they never really learn how to *make* money. Schools don't even teach us how to do this! But thankfully, I was lucky enough to learn a lot about making money from Bob Proctor. I learned that having multiple sources of income isn't just 'having another job'—it's not even a job at all! It should, instead, be made up of forms of income that come in *passively*, without you having to do anything to them. I learned many other things, all of which I'll be sharing with you throughout this book.

The bottom line is that I knew *nothing* about money. In fact, I grew up in an environment that only talked about the *lack* of money around, about *scarcity*. I was earning $7,200 a year when I started my career, then my income went to around $300K a year, and then it went to over a million. To this day, I've earned millions of dollars in my lifetime. I learned from the best, gained all their insights, and now, I want to share these with you throughout this book.

Once you can change your income, you can change *everything* in your life. You might not think that money's important—although I doubt that that's true, as you're reading this book—but I personally disagree. Money is incredibly important. It mightn't make you *happy*, but that's because it was never meant to. Money is meant to make us *comfortable*. It's needed so we can live freely without being worried about running out of it and living in an unstable situation. Money's there so we know we can access the things we need to access, and we don't have to worry about whether we'll be able to pay our rent in the coming months. Likewise, the more comfortable we are, the more we can be creative and think about *other ways* of making money.

Money is also there for us to use to help others. We want to *extend the good we do* far beyond our own physical presence. We want to do great things with that money. We want to be able to help people with that money. We want to be able to use that money to get a certain sense of safety and stability. So, to think that money isn't important is, in my perspective, foolish. The world runs on money, so saying that it isn't important is usually a defensive statement from a person who *doesn't have any*, and who doesn't know how to get any. Did you know that 1% of our population earns 99% of the world's wealth? Imagine if that number became more equitable.

Figure 1: The global wealth pyramid 2022

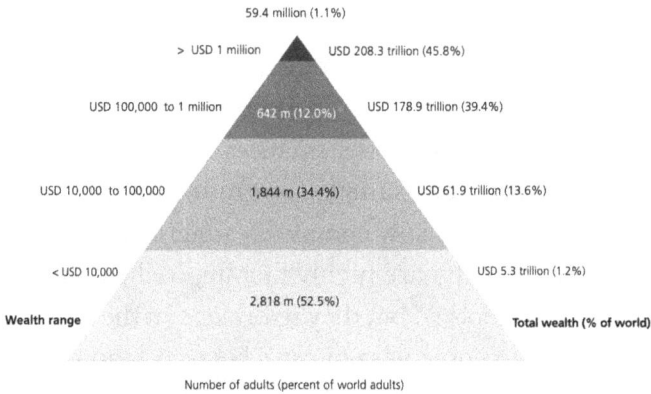

59.4 million (1.1%)

> USD 1 million · USD 208.3 trillion (45.8%)

USD 100,000 to 1 million · 642 m (12.0%) · USD 178.9 trillion (39.4%)

USD 10,000 to 100,000 · 1,844 m (34.4%) · USD 61.9 trillion (13.6%)

< USD 10,000 · USD 5.3 trillion (1.2%)

2,818 m (52.5%)

Wealth range · **Total wealth (% of world)**

Number of adults (percent of world adults)

Source: James Davies, Rodrigo Lluberas and Anthony Shorrocks, Global Wealth Databook 2023

One notable study that explored wealth distribution is the *Global Wealth Report* published annually by Credit Suisse Research Institute. This report provides valuable insights into global wealth distribution trends and highlights the concentration of wealth among the top percentile.

Here are some references to look into:

- Credit Suisse Global Wealth Report 2023: https://www.credit-suisse.com/about-us/en/reports-research/global-wealth-report.html
- Projections of Global Household Wealth: https://www.ubs.com/global/en/family-office-uhnw/reports/global-wealth-report-2023.html
- World Inequality Report 2022: https://wir2022.wid.world/www-site/uploads/2023/03/D_FINAL_WIL_RIM_RAPPORT_2303.pdf

Now, I'm a strong believer that earning money has nothing to do with intelligence. I have no formal business education, yet I earn over a million a year. However, the big part that many people are missing out on is **financial education**. We simply don't learn enough about finances in schools, and that's a major problem! For example, you most likely know many people who are financially completely illiterate. And then, we also have people who are highly literate, well-educated, and in the best of schools … but they're broke. On the other hand, you may know people who haven't been to school, yet now earn millions. There's no consistency, because of the lack of financial education in our schools. So, this is the book that aims to solve that problem. Throughout, I'll be teaching you how to make money and invest in yourself and your future. You're going to learn incredible things! And no, money has nothing to do with *work*. You see, we work for satisfaction, but we provide services to earn money. Keep this in mind as you move forward through the book!

One day, I woke up and realized that I didn't want to live like others, defined by society's narrow view of success as solely financial. While I'm immensely grateful for the wealth and lifestyle I've achieved, something was missing. My pursuit of greatness began, and I had to look for a bigger dream, a calling, a way to contribute to society. That's why I decided to write this book—to pass on my knowledge to others.

This book's about sharing hard-won knowledge with people like me who don't have networks or wealth, who are starting from scratch and trying to break free from being stuck.

I didn't come with a silver spoon in my mouth. I had to work hard, I had to learn, and I had to do it the hard way. I started from nothing, succeeded, failed, succeeded again, and navigated both corporate success and entrepreneurship. I've lived outside of my comfort zone.

Part of my success has been in identifying fear and replacing it with beliefs that can help you attain the success you desire.

I learned that we're victims of our subconscious mind, programmed human beings shaped by our environment, society, news, parents, and what we've been told about what we should or shouldn't do. The only way to break through is to reprogram ourselves into the humans we want to become, causing a shift in identity and personality—a transformation of our mindset.

I realized that I was stuck with my belief system, and came to understand that I could change it through the methods I'm going to reveal in this book to achieve greatness.

So, this book's for you. It was written for you, who wants to become financially independent. For you, who no longer wants to depend on your family. For you, who wants to finally be in control of your finances.

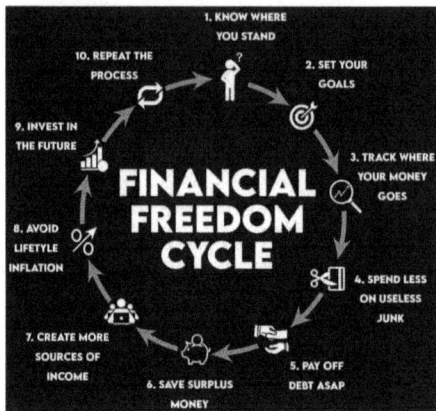

Here is an illustration to look at before we dig deeper. Let's get started!

What *is* Mindvestor? Here's what it means to me:

It's the MINDSET behind each INVESTOR, hence **MINDSET** stands for:

M—Motivation: A winning investor is driven by a strong motivation to succeed. They have clear goals and are willing to put in the necessary effort to achieve them.

I—Initiative: Taking initiative is key for someone with a winning mentality. They actively seek out opportunities, make informed decisions, and aren't afraid to take calculated risks.

N—Nimble: Being nimble means being adaptable and flexible in the face of changing market conditions. A winning investor knows how to quickly adjust their strategies and capitalize on emerging trends.

D—Discipline: Discipline is vital for managing investments effectively. It involves setting clear rules, sticking to a well-defined investment plan, and avoiding impulsive decisions based on emotions.

S—Strategic: A strategic investor thinks long-term and carefully plans their moves. They analyze market trends, assess risks, and make well-thought-out decisions that align with their overall investment objectives.

E—Education: Continuous learning is a hallmark of a winning investor's mindset. They stay informed about industry trends, seek out new knowledge and perspectives, and are always open to expanding their understanding of the markets they invest in.

T—Tenacity: This refers to the determination and perseverance required to overcome challenges and setbacks. A winning investor doesn't give up easily, but rather learns from failures and uses them as stepping stones towards future success.

By embracing the qualities represented by each letter of MINDSET, an investor can reflect a winning mentality that sets them apart in the financial, business, or real estate world.

INVESTOR stands for:

I—Intelligent: A successful investor possesses intelligence and makes informed decisions based on thorough research and analysis.

N—Nurturing: Good investors nurture their investments by actively monitoring and managing their portfolios, ensuring their long-term growth and success.

V—Visionary: Successful investors have a clear vision of their financial goals and develop strategies to achieve them, often thinking ahead of market trends.

E—Entrepreneurial & Experienced: Investors often have an entrepreneurial spirit, taking calculated risks to achieve financial gains. Experience plays a crucial role in successful investing. Seasoned investors have learned from past successes and failures, making them better equipped to navigate the complexities of the financial world.

S—Strategic: Investors need to be strategic in their decision-making process. They carefully evaluate risks and rewards, diversify their portfolios, and devise long-term plans to maximize returns.

T—Tenacious: Successful investors exhibit tenacity by staying focused on their objectives despite market fluctuations or setbacks. They remain committed to their investment strategies.

O—Opportunistic: Investors who excel in their fields are always on the lookout for opportunities. They have a keen eye for undervalued assets or emerging markets, enabling them to capitalize on potential gains.

R—Resourceful & Resilient: Successful investors are resourceful, utilizing their networks and expertise to gain insights and access to valuable resources. The ability to bounce back from setbacks is a defining quality of successful investors. They learn from failures, adapt their strategies, and remain resilient in the face of challenges.

By embodying these characteristics, an investor can navigate the financial, business, or real estate world with confidence and increase their chances of achieving their investment goals.

CHAPTER 1

GETTING UNSTUCK

*'DO WHAT YOU CAN WHERE YOU ARE
WITH WHAT YOU'VE GOT.'*

**—THEODORE ROOSEVELT (1858–1919),
26TH PRESIDENT OF THE UNITED STATES**

How does someone go from being a shopkeeper to becoming a major shareholder in a nine-figure company, building multiple sources of income trading the financial markets, and owning real estate, all in less than fifteen years? How does someone leave a war-torn region with nothing and find themselves with the world at their fingertips within such a short timeframe?

As I went from having nothing to achieving a life beyond my wildest dreams, I wouldn't have believed it possible. In the following chapters, I'll uncover all the methods, learnings, and strategies I employed to progress significantly in my personal and professional life.

I can assure you that it wasn't easy, and I had to step far out of my comfort zone. However, I can also assure you that it's entirely possible. If *I* could achieve it starting from scratch, anyone can do it.

By the end of this chapter, I will have laid out the journey I'm about to take you on and given you a glimpse of the keys to my success. It's my hope that these insights can help you reach your own heights. Success is inevitable if you want it enough and follow the science behind it, doing whatever it takes to align with your goals and dreams. You'll eventually reach your destination!

MINDSET SHIFT: WHAT IS IT?

Now, I understand that you may be wondering why this book starts with a discussion on mindset, considering that it's a book about reaching financial freedom. The reason's simple: You need to have the right mindset *before* you start working on your goals. You need to be ready to achieve whatever you might want to achieve and be ready to deal with the consequences or bad outcomes, whatever might happen. I didn't end up in this position while thinking about my situation as a terrible one, or by being a victim.

I recognize the significance of having the right mindset before embarking on any journey towards achieving goals, especially in the realm of financial freedom. By addressing mindset in the beginning, my aim is to emphasize its pivotal role in shaping one's actions and decisions.

It's important to recognize that success isn't solely achieved through practical strategies and techniques; it also requires a positive and determined mindset. Without the right mentality, it becomes difficult to overcome obstacles, maintain resilience, and stay motivated during challenging times.

Therefore, I'm highlighting my own experience as proof that adopting a proactive and empowered mindset can lead to financial freedom. I didn't reach my current position by dwelling on negativity and unfavorable circumstances. Instead, I took control of my thoughts and actions, which ultimately contributed to my success despite it involving a difficult journey.

It's important to understand that cultivating the right mindset is an essential foundation for achieving any goal, including financial independence.

I was constantly looking for ways out—out of poverty, out of this situation. I constantly wanted to be more, to do more, to achieve more. Your financial success will come as a result of all your hard work, but that hard work can only happen if you have a mindset that encourages you to put in all the hard work. If you don't care about the outcome, if you don't care about whether you can achieve those dreams, and if you don't believe in your potential, you aren't starting with the right mindset. You need to *believe* that you can succeed! You need to be ready to take all the hard steps that need to be taken, and to keep moving forward, even when the obstacles feel insurmountable!

Indeed, I'm a firm believer that success is all in the mind. Our belief systems either permit or disallow us from taking the next step. Always choose positive over negative thinking. I know, it's a lot more difficult to *do it* than to *say it*, but please trust me and do your best to focus on the positive, not the negative. Positive thinking will serve you, while negative thinking will hold you back. Focus on your future, *not your past*. A car is designed to look forward to reaching a destination, while rearview mirrors only serve you on your journey by displaying what's behind you. So, see your life this way as well. See your life with positive glasses on, instead of looking at it as a series of unfortunate events. You might be living in tough conditions, but it's up to you to ensure you aren't stuck in them forever, and ultimately move forward towards a better life.

There's never any magical circumstance that changes the trajectory of your life. Instead, an **internal switch** needs to happen. Realize that you have the power to create the life you want for yourself. You're in control. Your choices are yours, and so are the decisions you make every single day. Don't wait for your circumstances to change; change your circumstances.

I had nothing when I arrived from Beirut, just a dream of accomplishing something. I wanted to be a businessman, an entrepreneur. That was the picture in my mind. Similarly, your own journey has to start with a clear mind and a clear goal, a goal that must shake your existence and shape you while you're pursuing it. You have to think about it every single day, engrave it in your mind, picture it, and visualize it as if you're looking at a real view in front of your eyes. The more the picture in your mind becomes real, the more it becomes your reality.

Acknowledging the difficulty of changing your mindset is essential, as it's a common challenge that many individuals face. Shifting our perspectives, beliefs, and attitudes requires a great deal of effort and self-reflection. For some, this process can be particularly challenging, while for others, it may seem insurmountable. However, it's important to remember that **change isn't impossible**; it simply takes time and commitment. By understanding the hurdles that come with altering our mindset, we can approach the journey with patience and perseverance which will inevitably bring about the desired outcome we're seeking.

THE BIG PICTURE: THE HOW

How can you change your mindset and be more positive? Let's have a look. Personally, I use a pillar system. There are pillars that make up my life, and I can slowly work towards each of these. For example, one of the pillars is the **tactics, work ethics, and lessons** I've learned from mentorship. I wasn't always in the financial situation I'm in today, so I make sure to always return to the knowledge I've gained while learning from others who know more than I do.

Everything starts with how you see yourself and your belief system. So, work on your inner world to shine in your outer world. Here are a few strategies I cultivated to fortify my inner world:

- **Self-reflection**: Make an inventory of your thoughts, emotions, and behaviors. Write down all that's bothering you, then ask yourself why you behaved this way in that particular moment. What triggered you to behave in a certain way? Study yourself, find out why, then work on how to improve. Regular self-reflection helps you gain clarity about your inner self and allows you to make conscious choices aligned with your true desires.
- **Positive affirmations**: Use these to rewire your belief system. Repeat empowering statements about yourself regularly, such as 'I am capable', 'I am worthy', or 'I can achieve anything I set my mind to'. This practice helps build self-confidence and strengthens your self-belief.
- **Gratitude practice**: Develop a habit of expressing gratitude for the blessings in your life. Daily gratitude practice helps shift your focus towards positivity and enhances your overall wellbeing.
- **Journaling**: This was a big one for me, as it provides a safe space to explore your inner thoughts, feelings, and experiences. By putting pen to paper, you can gain valuable insights into your emotions, beliefs, and patterns of behavior. This self-reflection allows for personal growth and a deeper self-understanding, while helping you de-stress, gain clarity, and be creative.

- **Consistency** is constantly showing up and putting in the work, regardless of whether you have the talent to do something or not. As you consistently work on something, you'll inevitably get good at it.

Success is the sum of small efforts repeated every day. Imagine committing yourself to completing three to five important small steps or tasks every single day towards your dream goal. That's roughly twenty-one tasks a week, ninety tasks a month, 1100 tasks a year. That's how powerful this is.

Repetition is the mother of mastery. Therefore, rituals must be repeated every single day until they become automated. Once it's a habit, your cognition, energy, and productivity will triple. Your strength and willpower will be like iron. You'll be unstoppable.

Recover after hard work. Rest is important to recharge.

Likewise, another pillar is having **the right mindset for leadership and growth**. Now, you may not be in a leadership position. You may not be in charge of managing people or something similar, but you certainly *are* the leader of your own life. If you want to grow financially, if you want to get yourself out of an uncomfortable position, you *need* to have the right mindset for leadership and growth. That means being resilient when you're facing failures and knowing when to celebrate successes. It means taking action when needed and knowing *when* that action is needed—knowing when to take a certain action and when to change things up.

Another pillar is **investing in yourself so you can build a different future**. Thankfully, you're doing this right now! You need to be continuously investing in yourself *now*, so your future self can enjoy the hard work you've put in. It therefore also means you need to shift your mindset from being an *employee* to being an *employer*, because if you aren't paying other people, you're dependent on those who pay *you* to keep making money. You want it to come from your various business endeavors, not from a single person or company!

Likewise, **think about challenges as fuel**. Challenges enable me to consider how I can do things differently. They make me wonder whether I can do something better, or whether I could learn how to recover more efficiently. They make me think about how I can improve my current condition. They make me realize what I hold dear to my heart, because when something might be taken away from me, I realize how much I value it and how much I don't want to let it go. So, if you're currently in a challenging financial situation, take the time to consider what this situation might be teaching you. What can you gain from it?

Finally, I live by the pillar of **continuous learning**. In this day and age, there are countless new ways to make money. You can make money using your own skills, talents or gifts. You can invest in stocks, AI, Bitcoin, forex, real estate and many more ways. Not only this, but we're also living through highly volatile times, and we don't know what the future has in store for us. So, we need to protect ourselves. We need to make sure that we set up systems to protect ourselves from inflation. This is where continuous learning comes in—we need to continuously learn more about our circumstances. We have to continuously improve our knowledge and our skill set.

This is where this book comes in! It's about paying knowledge forward. It's about sharing the twenty-five years of hard work, sweat, and experience I've accumulated so I can provide you with all the tools, tactics, and methods I've developed throughout my career, hopefully inspiring *your* success.

This book's also about sharing my experiences, because knowledge is one part of the equation. What matters most is the implementation component, which is crucial as it reveals the process of getting from point A to point B. So, let's head over to the next chapter and start looking at how you can revamp your financial health.

CHAPTER 2

THE EVOLUTION OF FINANCIAL MARKETS

'I WILL TELL YOU HOW TO BECOME RICH. CLOSE THE DOORS. BE FEARFUL WHEN OTHERS ARE GREEDY. BE GREEDY WHEN OTHERS ARE FEARFUL.'

—WARREN BUFFETT

This quote was a turning point for me. It's opened my mind to new possibilities I'd never thought of. It suggested the importance of focusing on my own path and not being easily swayed by external influences. It encouraged me to shut out distractions and stay true to my own ambitions and goals.

It urged me to be cautious when others were overly eager and driven by greed. It reminded me to exercise prudence and not blindly follow the herd. When fear pervades the air, people often become hesitant and shy away from taking risks. However, this quote encouraged me to embrace a different approach. It advised me to be bold and seize opportunities when others are too afraid to do so.

If you look back to the Covid-19 days, and how the market crashed in 2020, *fear* offered a perfect explanation of how people started exiting their positions when this was actually the best opportunity to buy into the market for the long term. Soon enough, a year later the market bounced back; a few years later, you could've made a fortune by taking advantage of this situation.

In essence, Buffett's quote reminds me that wealth isn't just about luck or circumstance; it's also about having the right mindset and making strategic choices.

Now we've established the importance of having the right mindset when looking at your finances, let's start looking at how you can start acting on this mindset. First and foremost, I found it incredibly important to understand the financial market as a whole before I could even start working towards improving my finances. As I mentioned earlier, I had a lot to learn! So, I turned to mentors who could teach me, but I also had to do a *lot* of work to make sure I was up to date on all the knowledge that one must have. So, let's start with the very basics, which is the evolution of financial markets.

THE ORIGINS OF FINANCIAL MARKETS

The financial markets we know today aren't the same as those we used to know a few decades ago. The markets, before the rise of technology and digitalization, were characterized by much more pronounced informality. Then, technology came in and changed the game. We started trading not just items and products, but *stocks* too, which gave rise to all kinds of opportunities for individuals to grow their money. Human economic behavior changes all the time, and the switch from *physical marketplaces* to *digital trade* is just one example!

So, let's begin with a brief history lesson. Financial markets are nothing new. In fact, they can be traced back to the early days of civilization. Try picturing a marketplace that's full of people in Mesopotamia—it's not just goods that are being exchanged, but also IOUs, which is a phonetic match for 'I owe you', an informal way to promise that a debt will be repaid. Then, if we jump forward to 1602, the Amsterdam Stock Exchange was founded, officially becoming the first stock exchange. This was a complete game-changer, because businesses could raise capital by selling ownership stakes. Consequently, investors could share in the profits and risks. This might *seem* like a simple concept, but it seriously revolutionized our society's approach to money and profit-making.

We're now zooming into the 20th century. In the post–World War II era, we witnessed economic growth unlike anything we'd seen before (besides perhaps the Industrial Revolution). The middle class began to expand, and the stock market was becoming democratized. In other words, it was no longer just the playground of the elite—it could now be used by all with the means to purchase shares. It had become a public utility of sorts, and it was available to the average common people in town, instead of being reserved for the very richest.

Things once again took a turn in the late 20th and early 21st centuries, as technology began to play a significant role. For example, electronic trading in the 1970s revolutionized the markets by making them far more efficient and accessible. However, it also made them more complex. Today, we live in the age of high-frequency trading, with algorithms fighting one another on the digital battleground. Trades are now done in milliseconds, a far cry from the days of traders shouting orders on the stock exchange floor!

What we trade is also changing tremendously. A few decades ago, stocks and bonds were the main items being traded. Nowadays, this has changed significantly. ETFs, hedge funds, NFTs, crypto, derivatives … There are countless options for one to invest in the stock market. A few examples are listed here.

For those of you who'd like to know what the top hedge fund companies are, here's a list from the ETFDB website:
https://etfdb.com/compare/market-cap/

For those who'd like to know the top hedge fund companies, here's a list from Forbes:
https://www.forbes.com/advisor/investing/top-hedge-funds/

For those who'd like to know the top NFT companies, here's a list from Dappradar:
https://dappradar.com/rankings/nft/collections

For those who'd like to know the top Crypto companies, here's a list from Coinmarketcap:
https://coinmarketcap.com/

So, this gives you the possibility to lower your risk, leverage your assets, and make higher profits. However, more choice also brings more complexity, so trade at your own risk! You shouldn't be jumping into trading without having done your research and exercising due diligence—but that's what you're doing with this book!

We also saw significant events affecting the world. The dot com bubble in the 1990s, the 1970s oil crisis, the 2008 financial crisis, and more recently the Covid-19 pandemic that led to financial struggles all over the world due to high inflation—they *all* affected the way we spend money, and the way we *earn* it. Brexit wasn't helping things either, as it became difficult for many countries in the EU and others to trade with the UK without it costing them much more than previously. Now, we're in the middle of a transition period where we're seeing more pronounced changes than ever before. Advancements in AI, blockchain, and cryptocurrency are the future. They promise to redefine what markets look like and how they operate. So, you need to be ready!

WHAT DOES THIS MEAN FOR MY FUTURE?
WHAT YOU NEED TO KNOW

As we've seen, financial markets have seen a *lot* of changes and developments over the years. This has several implications for your future. You need to prepare yourself. The old ways of making money—namely starting a brick-and-mortar business and hoping for the best—are over. Now, you need to look at your other options, including how you can make money with the tools available to you *today*, and how to use these tools to build a *system* that makes you money, not just a system that makes you money *now*, but also in the *future*.

Consider the tools you have at your disposal, then think about how you can use these for the future.

Here are some of the tools I've used throughout my journey, and will keep on doing for many years to come:

1. **Online Trading Platforms**: Explore user-friendly platforms that allow you to invest in stocks, commodities, or cryptocurrencies from the comfort of your own home. These platforms offer real-time data, analytical tools, and educational resources to help you make informed investment decisions.
2. **Robo-Advisors**: Consider using automated investment services that employ algorithms to create and manage your investment portfolio. These services can provide personalized investment advice based on your goals, risk tolerance, and time horizon.

3. **Financial Apps**: Utilize mobile applications that offer budgeting, expense tracking, and investment management features. These apps can help you stay organized, monitor your spending habits, and make smarter financial decisions.

4. **Predictive Analytics Software**: AI-powered predictive analytics tools can forecast market trends, identify patterns, and provide insights into potential investment opportunities.

5. **Machine Learning Models**: Machine learning models can be trained on historical financial data to identify patterns and predict future market movements, assisting you in making smarter investment choices.

6. **Chatbots**: AI-powered chatbots can provide real-time customer support, answer queries about financial markets, and assist with trading activities.

7. **Online Learning Platforms**: Take advantage of educational resources available online to enhance your financial knowledge and skills. Platforms like Udemy or Coursera offer courses on various topics such as investing, entrepreneurship, or personal finance.

If you need more tailored advice or recommendations, you can always reach out to me through @serge.dfouni on Instagram.

These tools are designed to enhance your decision-making process and assist you in adapting to the changing landscape of financial markets while opening up exciting opportunities for your future success. Stay curious, embrace change, and be proactive in utilizing these tools to build a thriving financial system for yourself.

Most importantly, look at the past and spot common trends and patterns. What tends to be the pattern? What do you see happening throughout time? For example, what happens when wars like the one in Ukraine, and the more recent one in the Middle East, take place? How do these tend to impact the world economically?

Let's take the war in Ukraine with Russia, for example. During times of conflict, financial markets often experience increased volatility. This can be attributed to various factors such as uncertainty, geopolitical risks, and changes in global trade dynamics. Investors may become more cautious and seek safer assets, leading to shifts in asset prices and market sentiment.

In terms of specific trends and patterns, here are a few observations that have been noticed:

1. **Safe-Haven Assets**: During periods of geopolitical tension, investors often flock to safe-haven assets like gold, U.S. Treasury Bonds, or the Swiss Franc. These assets are perceived as more stable and tend to see increased demand, causing their prices to rise.
2. **Currency Fluctuations**: Wars and conflicts can impact currency values as they affect trade relations and investor confidence. Currencies of countries directly involved in

the conflict may experience depreciation due to economic disruptions, while currencies of countries perceived as safe havens may strengthen. For example, the US Dollar recently went through the roof in comparison with the Russian Ruble (RUB).

3. **Sector-Specific Impacts**: Certain sectors can be more sensitive to geopolitical events than others. For example, defense companies may see increased demand for their products and consequently experience stock price appreciation. On the other hand, industries heavily reliant on international trade (like oil, for example) may face challenges due to disruptions in supply chains or changes in global trade policies.

4. **Market Sentiment**: Geopolitical events can significantly influence market sentiment, creating waves of optimism or pessimism among investors. This sentiment can manifest in increased market volatility and fluctuations in stock prices.

Every challenge presents an opportunity for growth. By staying informed, remaining adaptable, and considering the potential impacts of significant events, you can position yourself to make sound financial decisions and navigate through changing economic landscapes. Keep your eyes open for emerging trends, as they often hold the key to unlocking new possibilities for your financial success.

It's important to note that each situation is unique and the impact on financial markets can vary. Therefore, it's crucial for investors to closely monitor the evolving situation and seek expert advice when making investment decisions.

Likewise, start thinking about how you could build wealth *over time*. Time will continue to run its course, whether we like it or not. It will continue to move forward, so whether you end up being a person who made money, or not, is what will make the difference. Look at the information you have, then deduct things from this. What can you learn to do better? How can you use current circumstances to improve your financial situation? How can you use emerging technologies, or trends, to make money? The richest individuals, whether they're Bezos or Musk, jumped on the opportunity to be *different* and offer something that no one had ever thought of offering before. So, be like them!

Jeff Bezos, the founder of Amazon, is a great example of someone who saw the potential in the emerging market for online sales. He recognized that the internet would revolutionize the way people shop and saw an opportunity to create a platform that would cater to this growing trend. By jumping on this opportunity at an early stage, Bezos was able to build Amazon into the global powerhouse it is today.

Elon Musk, on the other hand, has made several groundbreaking moves in different industries. One notable example is his involvement in creating PayPal, a digital payment system that simplified money transfers between individuals. Musk recognized the importance of making financial transactions more accessible and convenient for people.

Additionally, Musk saw another emerging market: electric cars. He understood the need for sustainable transportation and was the first to launch Tesla, an innovative electric car company. By being ahead of the curve and taking risks in uncharted territories, Musk has become a trailblazer in the automotive industry.

Both Bezos and Musk exemplify visionary entrepreneurs who possess a keen eye for identifying emerging markets and seizing opportunities. Their success not only stems from their ability to recognize these trends, but also from their determination to take action and turn their visions into reality.

Remember, it's always inspiring to see individuals who have the foresight to embrace change, take risks, and create something extraordinary. To capitalize on such opportunities in the financial markets, it's important to stay informed about emerging trends and industries. Conduct thorough research, analyze market data, and contemplate long-term prospects before making investment decisions. Remember, success often comes to those who can anticipate future needs and adapt accordingly.

THE WINNING WALLET MENTALITY

*'IN INVESTING, WHAT IS COMFORTABLE
IS RARELY PROFITABLE.'*

—ROBERT ARNOTT

At Winning Wallet Trading, the company I founded in the hopes of helping, guiding, and equipping traders and investors with education, tools, and AI software in order to make informed decisions when trading the financial markets, we help you think about your future. So, let me tell you a bit more about what we do, and how we could help you. Our goal is to give you a solid investment that's secure, safe, and provides high returns in a *small period of time.* It can provide up to 20–50% return yearly—don't trust me? I've done it, and I can show you *how.*

Let's imagine that you invest $1M. That's roughly $200–$500K *return* in a year. If you keep your $1M intact, your investment will grow. The longer you keep the investment (for two, three, or five years, for example), the more your investment will grow. In five years, this same $1M can become $10M.

This example can be applied to any investment size, depending on your current stage in the investment journey. Whether it's $10K, $30K, $50K or any other amount, the decision ultimately depends on your risk appetite. For instance, if you're comfortable with taking on more risk and are open to using leverage ratios like 1:20, 1:100, or even 1:500, the potential rewards can be significant and realized quickly. However, it's important to note that higher leverage also comes with increased risk. Ultimately, the choice is yours to make based on your own preferences and risk tolerance.

Here are some examples to illustrate the points I mentioned:

'Imagine making a small investment of just $5,000 and seeing it grow exponentially. With the right strategy and market knowledge, your initial investment could be 5x, 10x or even 30x. Whether you're starting small or have a larger budget of $10,000 or even $30,000, the potential for profit is within reach.'

Or: 'Are you someone who thrives on taking calculated risks? By leveraging your investment with ratios like 1:20, 1:100, or even 1:500, you have the opportunity to amplify your gains and reap incredible rewards. Picture the excitement of seeing your investment multiply at lightning speed. However, it's important to remember that higher leverage also means higher risk. It's a decision that should be made based on your risk appetite and careful consideration.'

'The power to choose your investment journey lies in your hands. Whether you prefer a more conservative approach or are willing to embrace higher risks for potentially greater returns, the choice is yours. With investments tailored to suit your risk appetite and leverage options to match, you have the freedom to shape your financial future according to your preferences and goals.'

But the problem that you might have encountered over the past few years is that once you put money in, you might not see returns coming back to you *quickly*. Instead, you know you need to wait for many, many more than five years to see that initial investment grow to that level. So what's different with us? We'll have a closer look at this throughout the next few chapters.

What we're offering you is the **holy grail** of investing. We offer you great investments, less risk, and great returns. The big difference? We don't use leverage to avoid losses and capital depreciation and we capitalize on AI and machine learning to win the game and make the difference.

I always recommend adopting a risk–reward ratio in your trading (this refers to the potential gain versus potential loss of a trade). It's a crucial concept you can use to assess the profitability and riskiness of their trades. A 3:1 risk–reward ratio, for example, means that for every unit of risk taken, you can expect to make three units of profit.

Let's consider an example to better understand this concept. Suppose you decide to buy a stock at $50 per share, with a stop-loss order set at $48 and a take-profit order at $56.

In this scenario, you're risking $2 per share (the difference between the entry price and the stop-loss price) and aiming for a profit of $6 per share (the difference between the take-profit price and the entry price).

If you're wondering what a stop-loss order is, it's a risk management tool used in trading to protect investors from potential losses, in the form of an instruction given to a broker or exchange to sell a security if it reaches a predetermined price level. The purpose of a stop-loss order is to limit the amount of loss an investor may incur on a trade. By setting a stop-loss level, investors can automatically exit a position and minimize their losses if the market moves against them. This order type is widely used by traders to manage risk and ensure they stay within their predetermined risk tolerance levels.

WHAT IS A
STOP LOSS?

ENTRY

RISK

STOP LOSS

THE STOP LOSS IS A PRICE LEVEL THAT
THE TRADE WILL CLOSE AUTOMATICALLY.

IT IS IMPORTANT TO USE A STOP LOSS AS IT WILL LIMIT THE RISK
ON A TRADE. IF A STOP LOSS IS NOT USED IT CAN LEAD TO A
LARGER THAN NECESSARY LOSS.

Olga Forex

If the trade goes in your favor, reaching the take-profit level would get you a profit of $6 per share, while your potential loss would be limited to $2 per share if the trade hits the stop-loss level. Therefore, the risk–reward ratio in this example would be 3:1, as the potential reward is three times greater than the potential risk.

Another example could be in forex trading. Let's say you decide to enter a currency trade with an initial risk of 50 pips and aim for a reward of 150 pips. In this case, if the trade reaches the desired target, you'd achieve a threefold increase in profit compared to your initial risk.

Are you wondering what a pip is? Short for 'percentage in point', it's a unit of measurement used in forex trading to quantify the change in value between two currencies.

It represents the smallest incremental movement a currency pair's exchange rate can make. Typically, a pip is equal to 0.0001 for most currency pairs (except for those involving the Japanese Yen, where it's 0.01). Pips are crucial for calculating profits and losses in forex trading and serve as a reference point for determining price movements.

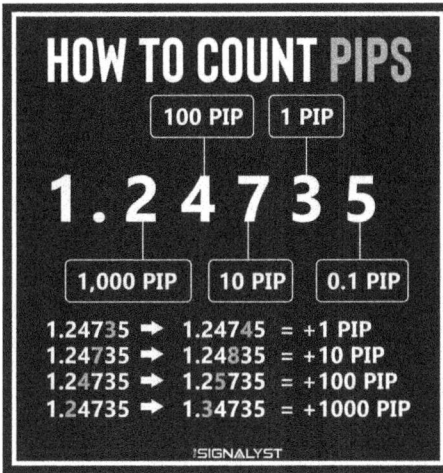

By favoring a 3:1 risk–reward ratio, you aim to have higher potential profits compared to your potential losses. This approach allows you to have fewer winning trades while still maintaining profitability overall.

It's important to note that while a 3:1 ratio can be favorable, it may not be achievable in all trading situations. Each trade should be assessed individually based on market conditions, volatility, and other factors that may affect the risk–reward ratio.

Let's say you're considering buying shares of XYZ Company at $50 per share. You believe the stock price could rise to $70 in the near future, giving you a potential profit of $20 per share. However, you also acknowledge that if the stock price drops, you may need to cut your losses and sell at $45 per share, resulting in a potential loss of $5 per share.

In this scenario, the risk–reward ratio would be 20/5, or 4:1. This means that for every $1 you stand to lose, you have the opportunity to gain $4. This indicates a favorable risk–reward ratio, which may make the trade more appealing to you.

In conclusion, the risk–reward ratio in trading is a vital component in assessing the profitability and riskiness of a trade. However, it's essential to adapt this ratio to individual trading strategies and market conditions for optimal decision-making.

That's right—you get to keep your money in your brokerage account under **your** control. All we do is trade it for you on your behalf.

CHAPTER 3

BUILDING A WEALTH MINDSET

*'AN INVESTMENT IN KNOWLEDGE
PAYS THE BEST INTEREST.'*

—BENJAMIN FRANKLIN

So, you want to level up your life. You want to reach financial success. This is great news! Do you have the right mindset? In the first chapter, we started looking at how to get yourself unstuck. Now, let's home in on how to use that mindset for financial growth specifically. Everything in your life comes down to the choices you're making, and whether these choices are good for your life or not. It all comes down to how you use your assets. **And if you *already* have a lot of wealth, but don't know what to do with it yet or feel like you've been mismanaging it, this chapter's especially important for you!**

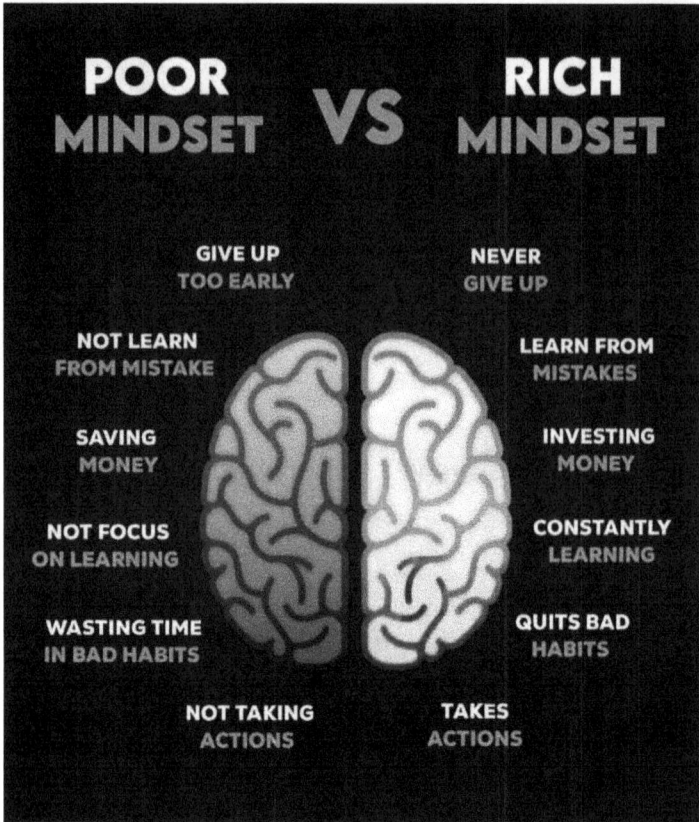

POOR MINDSET VS RICH MINDSET

GIVE UP TOO EARLY — NEVER GIVE UP

NOT LEARN FROM MISTAKE — LEARN FROM MISTAKES

SAVING MONEY — INVESTING MONEY

NOT FOCUS ON LEARNING — CONSTANTLY LEARNING

WASTING TIME IN BAD HABITS — QUITS BAD HABITS

NOT TAKING ACTIONS — TAKES ACTIONS

TAKE THE HARDER PATH

Easy choices lead to a difficult life, while hard choices lead to an easier life. This includes taking hard actions, making tough decisions, and engaging in challenging communication. Your dream life awaits on the other side of discomfort. So, step out of your comfort zone, as the hard route's the only one worth taking. It's understandable that stepping outside your comfort zone will feel uncomfortable. However, what would you prefer: Feeling uncomfortable for a short period of time, then living your dream life for a lifetime … or staying stuck where you are and regretting missing out on the life you've always wanted for the rest of your life?

In my case, I made a bold decision to embark on a challenging journey. I chose to step out of my comfort zone by leaving my country, family, and friends behind to establish a new life in Dubai. This hard choice demonstrated my determination and commitment to personal growth.

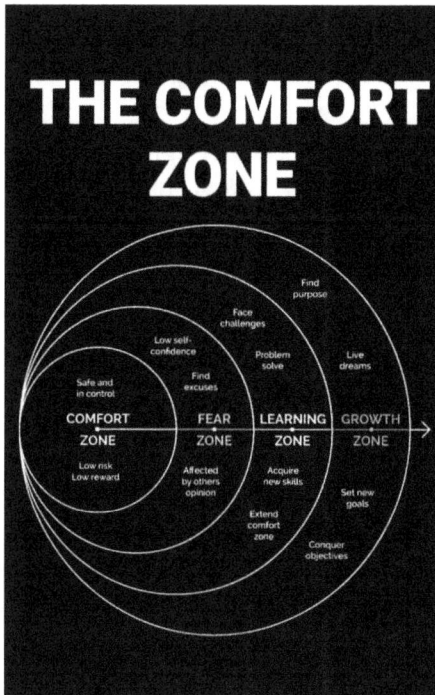

I opted for the hard path, which involved climbing the ladder of success through dedication and hard work. By putting in long hours and investing my weekends to learn and impress my superiors, I displayed a strong work ethic and a hunger for knowledge. Instead of settling for mediocrity or taking the easy way out, I took risks that pushed me outside of my comfort zone.

My willingness to embrace uncertainty and pursue opportunities with calculated risks set me apart. While others may have played it safe, I recognized the importance of venturing into uncharted territory to achieve personal and professional growth. This fearless attitude has likely contributed to my success in various aspects of my life, including my career and investments.

Moreover, I demonstrated foresight by focusing on long-term goals rather than being swayed by short-term gains. By playing the patience game, I exhibited a deep understanding that success takes time and perseverance. This strategic approach is commendable, as it shows I have the vision to make decisions based on long-term benefits rather than instant gratification.

If you want to become a leader in your own life, and if you want to make more money and get the financial freedom that comes with it, you can't choose the easiest path each time. You have to take the harder path sometimes, because this is where growth can happen. This also means using the assets you have in a *smart way*.

USE THE ASSETS YOU HAVE

Your biggest asset is your **brain**. Your mind controls your *life*, your *success*, your *career*, and your *relationships*. Your brain is the reason you're able to succeed. It's the reason you can achieve the great things you dream of achieving. So use it well! Use it to the fullest of its capacity. Remember, the quality of your thoughts determines the quality of your life. You need to know how to use this asset well to make the most out of it.

And look, it's something we all have to learn. In my late teens and early twenties, I began to assess the people around me. My parents were doing their best but were stuck in challenging circumstances. I had to realize that no one was going to change for me, and no one was going to give me a helping hand. If I were to reach my dreams, it was entirely up to me. I yearned to break free from that reality, but I understood that no one would show me the way. I had to realize that it was entirely up to *me* to use *my assets* in a smart way. No one else was going to do it for me!

It was a truly remarkable moment of my life where I felt I had within me the asset holding the key to my success, career, and relationships. By acknowledging this, I felt I was one step ahead in harnessing the full potential of my brain, and hence my life.

The great news is, I realized I had control over my mind after reading the book *The Secret*, and can shape my thoughts to create the life I desire. When you utilize your brain to its fullest capacity, you unlock endless possibilities for personal growth and achievement.

By understanding that the quality of your thoughts directly impacts the quality of your life, you've taken an important first step towards maximizing this invaluable asset. Now, it's time to explore strategies and techniques to effectively use your brain to your advantage.

Consider investing in activities that stimulate your mind, such as reading books, engaging in thought-provoking conversations, continuously learning, improving yourself, and developing new skills. Make a conscious effort to replace negative thoughts with positive ones and practice gratitude regularly. Surround yourself with uplifting and inspiring individuals who encourage your personal and professional development.

Remember, your brain's not only a tool for success but also a source of innovation and creativity. For me, it was my superpower!

THE WORK MUST COME FROM YOU

Have you ever felt, in your youth, that something magical was going to happen in your life? That someone would offer you the keys to success, or an event would change the course of your life? Eventually, you wake up and realize that it's just a fairytale. Internal preparation is required. **The work must start from the inside out.** The inner world must be primed for success. You need to read, and you need to culti-vate the right mindset. This is why I read books like *Think and Grow Rich*, because they gave me the knowledge I needed to really succeed. They showed me what I needed to know to stop thinking about making money in the *short term* and start thinking about how to make money in the *long term* instead. I also learned a lot from Robin Sharma, who had a profound impact on my life.

I learned about the element of influence called PENAM, which is about how your parents, environment, nation, associations, and media all influence who you are and become. (You can read an overview of PENAM at https://www.rismedia.com/2024/05/03/thoughts-leadership-penam-architectural-forces-shaping-you/.)

Parents play a significant role in shaping your decision-mak-ing processes due to the influence of their upbringing, cul-ture, and beliefs. However, it's important to remember that while these factors are influential, they don't have to dictate your choices entirely. By acknowledging and understanding the impact of parental influence, you can take steps to criti-cally evaluate your decisions and beliefs.

To gain a positive outcome from this situation, you can engage in open and honest conversations with your parents to express your own thoughts and perspectives. It's essential to commu-nicate openly about how parental influences may be affecting your decision-making and work towards finding a balance between honoring your heritage and deciding your own path.

Seeking guidance from mentors or counselors can also be beneficial in gaining a fresh perspective and developing independent decision-making skills. Additionally, exploring different perspectives, cultures, and beliefs through travel, education, or social interactions can help broaden your mindset and cultivate a more diverse approach to decision-making.

You have to be mindful of parental influences and actively work towards personal growth and self-awareness, as with greater clarity and confidence you can achieve positive outcomes.

Creating a positive **environment** can significantly enhance your overall wellbeing and productivity. Start by decluttering and organizing your living space and work area to promote a sense of calm and focus. Incorporate elements of nature, such as plants or natural light, to boost your mood and creativity. Ensure that you drink clean, fresh water and breathe in clean air by maintaining good ventilation and air quality in your surroundings.

Additionally, consider incorporating mindfulness practices or relaxation techniques into your daily routine to manage stress and enhance mental clarity. Regular physical activity and a balanced diet can also contribute to your health and energy levels, allowing you to work towards your goals with greater efficiency and enthusiasm.

By consciously creating a supportive environment that nurtures your physical, mental, and emotional wellbeing, you can positively influence your mindset, health, and productivity, ultimately empowering you to achieve success in various aspects of your life.

A positive environment will change the way you feel about yourself. It affects your health, and hence can affect your ability to work hard towards reaching your goals.

Your **nation** also affects this. Some nations have restrictions that hinder greatness or possess cultures and mentalities that don't serve your goals. For example, I had to leave Beirut because I didn't feel like it was serving me anymore. Lebanon wouldn't allow me to reach my dreams and goals, so I had to put myself first and get out while I could. I understand that this isn't always possible, and that sometimes you don't have the opportunity to just move away because of passport restrictions—but if you indeed see that your country is the reason why you can't work towards your goals, and the reason why you're likely to end up stuck where you are, you need to get yourself out of there. You have to make this a priority!

Next, your **associations**, such as your workplace and organizations, play a significant role in shaping your life. They can greatly impact your mindset, beliefs, and ultimately who you become. It's important to recognize the influence these environments have on you.

To ensure a positive outcome from your associations, it's crucial to actively assess and choose environments that align with your values and goals. If your current work or organization is fostering a fixed mindset and negatively affecting your wellbeing, consider the following steps I implemented to improve my situation:

Self-reflection: Take time to reflect on how your current associations are influencing you. Identify any negative patterns or beliefs that may be hindering your personal growth.

Seeking support: Reach out to mentors, colleagues, or friends who can provide guidance and support as you navigate challenging work environments.

Professional development: Invest in opportunities for growth and learning within your field. This can help you develop a growth mindset and expand your skills and knowledge.

Networking: Build connections with individuals who share similar values and aspirations. Surrounding yourself with positive influences can help counteract the negative effects of toxic work environments.

Exploring new opportunities: If necessary, consider exploring new job opportunities or organizations that better align with your values and goals. Don't be afraid to make a change if it means improving your overall wellbeing and mindset.

You have the power to choose the associations that shape your life. By being proactive and intentional in selecting environments that support your growth and development, you can create a more positive and fulfilling path for yourself.

The **media**, with the news it shares, can change the way we perceive the world. The news tends to focus on chaos, drama, disruptions, and negativity, instead of focusing on things that are more positive and can add to your life. So, while that doesn't mean you should avoid watching the news at all costs, it *does* mean you should be paying attention to the kind of content you consume and how it's affecting your perspective. It's all in your mindset—if you feel defeated, and if you feel like you can't change your circumstances because all you hear about is how negative everything is, change the kind of content you're listening to.

In my case, I limit exposure to negative news. While staying informed is important, I considered setting boundaries on how much negative news I consume to maintain a balanced view. I also engage with solutions-oriented content and look for news sources that highlight solutions to problems rather than just focusing on the issues themselves.

All I'm saying is, be mindful of the content you engage with and make conscious choices about what you consume; you can take control of your media diet and cultivate a more balanced and positive outlook on the world.

The point is, all these factors can have a negative impact on your life, your belief system, and your perception of the world. To rewire your future or change these elements of PENAM, you must build awareness, recognize these factors, and internally shift your perspective to achieve positive outcomes.

These factors influence you on a deep subconscious level, so it's crucial to be aware of them, bring to the surface what isn't serving you, and make the decision to change. In my case, I had to leave behind my parents, my living environment, my job, my friends, and even my country, as these factors weren't serving me, and I would've remained stuck had I not made the decision to move.

THE PILLARS TO A SUCCESSFUL AND HAPPY LIFE

In building a wealth mindset, you need to have several pillars that support all your efforts. This mindset is the lens through which you perceive and interpret the world around you. A positive and growth-oriented mindset can empower you to overcome challenges, achieve your goals, and find financial stability in your life. The goal is to adopt a mindset that makes you goal-oriented, encourages you to embrace challenges (even if they feel insurmountable), and allows you to grow tremendously as a result.

The first pillar is your **emotions and feelings**, including fears, anger, sadness, happiness, nervousness, and jealousy, among many others. If you want to succeed financially, you can't just focus on the money. You can't just focus on achieving goals and material success. You need to embrace emotionality and a heartfelt mindset. This helps you enhance your relationship. It promotes emotional wellbeing, guides decision-making, builds resilience, brings meaning and purpose, and fuels creativity. By prioritizing your emotions alongside your mindset, you can unlock your full potential and experience a truly rewarding life.

Practicing mindfulness and self-awareness helped me a lot. By being in tune with my emotions and understanding how they impact my decisions and behaviors, I can make more informed choices that benefit my financial goals.

For example, when I first started off my corporate career, I decided to challenge my tendency to feel jealous of my more experienced peers' success at work. Instead of letting my emotions fester and potentially harm my professional relationships, I could acknowledge the jealousy, understand its root cause, and use it as motivation to improve my own skills and performance. This not only fostered my personal growth but also enhanced my chances of succeeding financially in the long run.

So I chose to join them by being very supportive and helpful, learning from them and focusing on the business performance rather than my emotions and feelings so I could navigate challenges more effectively, build stronger connections with them, and ultimately achieve greater financial success.

The second pillar is your **soul and spirituality**. This includes being kind, looking for peace, living blissfully, and being joyful, pure, divine, creative, and loving. Connect to your true self so you know exactly what you're looking for in life, and why this is connected to financial wellbeing. Know what kind of financial wellbeing you're looking for—is it financial stability? Wealth? Being incredibly rich?

I started taking action on nurturing my soul and spirituality early in my career when I began prioritizing and planning my morning routine to connect with my inner self. I was committed to setting aside time each day to reflect on my values, goals, and desires, so I could gain clarity on what truly brings me joy and fulfillment.

For instance, I begin each morning by setting aside ten to fifteen minutes for quiet reflection and journaling. I use this time to express gratitude, set intentions for the day ahead, and visualize the kind of life I aspire to lead. This practice helped me align my actions with my values, leading to a greater sense of purpose and contentment in both my personal and my financial pursuits.

The third pillar is your **health**, which includes your fitness, vitality, energy, strength, and wellbeing. This pillar promotes emotional wellbeing, guides decision-making, builds resilience, brings meaning and purpose, and fuels creativity. By prioritizing your emotions alongside your mindset, you can unlock your full potential and experience a truly rewarding life. Without good health, you have nothing. You can't work properly. You can't motivate yourself to do well. You can't find the energy to get anything done. So, you *need* your health. You might be tempted to work overtime, skip sleep, and put your health on the backburner for the sake of making money, but once your health is out the window, that's it. There's nothing coming in anymore. So, exercise, eat well, and give yourself the time and space to sleep and rest.

By engaging in physical activities, you promote emotional wellbeing through the release of endorphins, which are known to reduce stress and improve mood. I found that very helpful for my situation, as my daily workout takes out all the stress of the day and boosts my energy and mood.

For instance, making time for a daily workout routine can significantly impact your mental clarity and decision-making abilities. You may find that after exercising, you feel more focused and motivated to tackle challenges with a positive mindset. Additionally, the discipline and commitment required for maintaining a consistent exercise regimen can build resilience and perseverance, helping you navigate life's obstacles with greater ease.

By prioritizing your health and emotional wellbeing through regular exercise, you not only enhance your physical capabilities but also fuel creativity and find deeper meaning and purpose in your daily life. Ultimately, investing in your health empowers you to unlock your full potential and lead a truly rewarding life filled with vitality and productivity. Remember, without good health, it becomes challenging to perform at your best both personally and professionally.

By taking action to care for your physical health, you're investing in your emotional wellbeing and setting the stage for a more fulfilling and productive life. Remember, a healthy body supports a healthy mind, enabling you to thrive in all aspects of your life.

The fourth pillar is your **mindset**, which we've discussed in detail. To recap, you need to cultivate a positive mindset. Believe in yourself and your abilities. Embrace a can-do attitude that will propel you forward even in the face of challenges. Remember, your thoughts have a direct impact on your actions and results. If you don't constantly challenge yourself, you risk becoming stagnant. Pushing beyond your comfort zone is essential for personal and professional growth. Seek out opportunities that stretch your capabilities and encourage continuous learning.

BODY
Physical Dimension
- Exercise
- Eat Healthy
- Sleep | Rest
- Relaxation

MIND
Mental Dimension
- Read
- Educate
- Write
- Learn new skills

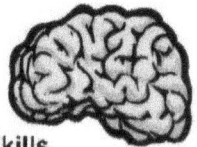

HEART
Emotional Dimension
- Build Relationships
- Give Service
- Laugh | Love

SOUL
Spiritual Dimension
- Meditate
- Keep a Journal
- Pray
- Take in Quality Media

TOOLS FOR A BETTER MINDSET

To achieve this, try using tools like visualization, positive affirmations, and meditation.

Visualization is a powerful tool that enhances goal-setting, motivation, problem-solving, performance, and creativity. By harnessing the power of mental imagery, you can bring your goals and ideas to life, paving the way for success in various areas of your life. I was visualizing different things at different periods of my life, whether it was the woman I wanted to date, the relationships I wanted to have, the money, the career, the business, the sports car, or the house I wanted to live in. It all started with me having a picture in my mind and holding that picture every single day. What are the pictures you have in your mind?

Positive affirmations play a significant role in your life, as they have the power to shape your thoughts, your beliefs, and ultimately your actions. By repeating positive statements about yourself and your goals, you can reprogram your subconscious mind to align with your desires—financial security, wealth, etc. This practice helps instill a sense of confidence, motivation, and self-belief, enabling you to overcome your challenges and achieve success. Choose words for your affirmations that tie into your goal, remembering that repetition is key. Mixing repetition and emotion when saying your affirmations, reading them out loud in front of a mirror, recording them on your phone, setting them as reminders, writing them down repeatedly, and creating a vision board for your goal can all be effective methods.

'I am' affirmations offer the strongest powers and forces that allow you to reach your goals. When you use 'I am' to start your affirmations, it works in attracting all the good things to you and allows you to forgive and have a forgiving heart towards those people who wronged you.

I also recommend writing or speaking your affirmation in the present tense.

This helps you to believe that the statement is true *right now*. For instance, 'I am well-prepared and well-rehearsed, and I can give a great presentation' would be a great affirmation to use if you feel nervous speaking in front of a group.

Or try, 'I'm so grateful now that money comes to me easily and effortlessly on a continuous basis through multiple sources of income' if you want to bring financial abundance to your life.

Meditation is a powerful practice that holds immense importance in today's fast-paced and stressful world. It allows you to find a moment of peace, stillness, and self-reflection amidst the chaos of your daily life. Incorporating meditation into your everyday routine can bring about profound positive changes. Whether it's dedicating a few minutes each day or attending guided meditation sessions, the benefits are well worth the effort, impacting your mental wellbeing, physical health, emotional balance, productivity, and overall wellbeing—all backed up by science and studies. You need to have your head on your shoulders to be able to take care of yourself financially, and meditation can help you with this.

I typically enjoy practicing meditation while listening to my favorite meditative music from my playlist, accompanied by the soothing aroma of frankincense essence to enhance the overall experience.

I like Mindfulness meditation, which originates from Buddhist teachings and is the most popular and researched form of meditation in the West. In mindfulness meditation, you pay attention to your thoughts as they pass through your mind.

Use these simple steps to start meditating:

- Find a comfortable spot where you can relax.
- Set a timer for three to five minutes.
- Begin by focusing on your breath. …
- As soon as your thoughts begin to wander, acknowledge the thoughts that come up, let them go, and return your focus to your breathing. …
- When your time's up, open your eyes.

Meditation can offer general health and mental/emotional benefits, including:

- lower blood pressure
- reduced stress

- better sleep
- improved emotional regulation
- increased focus
- enhanced mood
- reduced aggression
- greater adaptability
- a healthier aging process
- a greater sense of empathy and connection with others.

MAKING MONEY WHILE YOU SLEEP

Next on our list is the creation of *passive income*. If you're a seasoned investor, you already know all about it. If you're new to this world, let me introduce it to you. Passive income is the very process through which your money *makes you money*. It's how you turn money into *wealth*, because you make your assets continue to create more value. Personally, I learned early on in my financial journey that passive income was the way to go. This is because you have two options in life if you want to continue building wealth: to make a very high hourly wage, or to make money without needing to spend time on it. Which one would you prefer? I had experiences where I didn't make much money. I had times in my life when I barely made ends meet. But thankfully, this ended, and now, I know that I can't only rely on earning a wage from *working*– most of my income comes from passive sources!

So, you want to make money. As just mentioned above, you have two options: Either you make a *lot* per hour, or you make money while you sleep. Most of us prefer the latter option! Passive income isn't only how you make more money—it's especially related to how you create a safety net for yourself. What if you were to lose your job? What if something went wrong? This is why you need a form of passive income—a way for you to keep making money even if your main source of income diminishes.

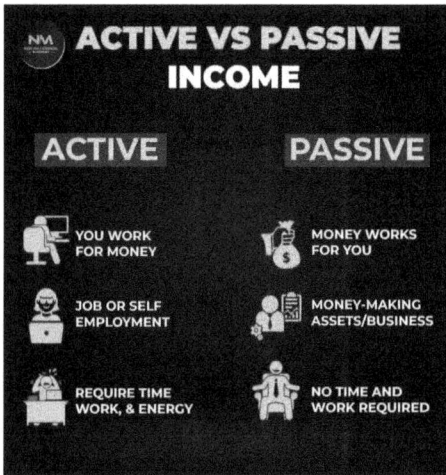

SOURCES OF PASSIVE INCOME TO EXPLORE

There are many sources that you may want to explore. For example, start by looking into real estate investments, which can range from rental properties to investment in real estate trusts (REITs). Otherwise, you may be interested in exploring dividend stocks, which we'll discuss in much more detail throughout the next few chapters. Alternatively, you could create digital products or develop an automated business or venture. The idea is that you should invest in *many different things*, to ensure you don't put all your eggs into one basket. However, the focus has to always remain on your main business or primary source of income.

BALANCING *SHORT-TERM* GAINS WITH *LONG-TERM* WEALTH-BUILDING

Creating **wealth** isn't just about immediate returns. It's primarily a long game. It involves balancing the *allure* of short-term gains with the necessity of long-term planning. So, it involves mixing short-term investments, like stocks, cryptocurrencies, or high-yield savings accounts, which often bring **quick returns**. Then, you also want long-term investments, like retirement accounts or index funds, because they grow *over time*, and help you benefit from compound interest. The investment I made in 2010 is now almost 200x my money over that period of fourteen years. To give you an example: If your investment was $10,000, the return would be $2M. If your investment was $100,000, the return would be a staggering $20M. How about if the investment was $1M? You would be looking at a return of $200M. That's the power of compounding your money and letting it grow over a period of time.

The balance is where you need to get the right mix to have the right portfolio. For example, you might have a portion of your portfolio allocated to stock trading for short-term gains, but another large part invested in more long-term and stable assets. The exact balance, however, depends on the kind of investor you are, which we'll discuss soon.

Ultimately, for you to be able to amass true wealth, you need to have the mindset that comes along with it. Don't focus on what's going wrong or what you don't have—look at what you *do* have instead. Get yourself out of the scarcity mindset. Lean into the things that make you feel scared, because greatness comes from the consistent doing of hard things and the discomfort of growth is always to be preferred over the illusion of safety. Welcome these challenging times, as well as the growth that comes along with them. Be *excited* about the path ahead, not scared of it! On that note, let's head over to the next chapter.

Avoid a scarcity mindset and embrace the unknown with courage. Welcome challenges that may seem daunting, as true success comes from consistently tackling difficult tasks. Choose the discomfort of personal growth over retaining a false sense of security.

For instance, rather than dwelling on financial limitations, concentrate on your existing skills, experiences, and resources that can potentially propel you towards wealth accumulation. By taking calculated risks and stepping out of your comfort zone, you open yourself up to new opportunities for growth and success. This proactive approach can ultimately lead to the development of a wealthy mindset and pave the way for achieving financial prosperity.

In my case, despite facing numerous rejections and setbacks when launching my first hospitality business or when I started investing in the financial markets, I remained focused on my vision and strengths. I embraced challenges and pushed past my comfort zone, eventually building a nine-figure business and passive income streams.

CHAPTER 4

MASTERING RISK AND REWARD

*'THE BIGGEST RISK IS NOT TAKING ANY RISK ...
IN A WORLD THAT'S CHANGING REALLY QUICKLY,
THE ONLY STRATEGY THAT IS GUARANTEED TO FAIL
IS NOT TAKING RISKS.'*

—MARK ZUCKERBERG

When I started trading five years ago, I thought I could make money trading the financial markets by just listening to advisors on the news and getting advice from here and there. However, *nothing* was working, and I was constantly losing! Of course, this isn't where you want to be in life, and it's not an ideal financial situation to be in.

My dream at that point was to be financially free and generate additional sources of passive income, but I wasn't really making any money, and I was addicted to returning the money—only to be losing *more and more.*

It took until I lost almost **$650K** to realize that I was doing things wrong.

I was only relying on my emotions, reading the news, and gaining little to no experience. The anger, shame, and frustration gave me the fuel I needed to learn and educate myself! I was committed to succeeding, and I wanted to learn from the *best*—and that meant getting myself a mentor. So, I started taking courses and met a mentor—the person who's now my partner, and who taught me everything I know today!

I started using those tools and AI software solutions, then started to make consistent profits on a monthly basis. I started educating myself in trading, and realized I needed the knowledge to be successful. I was *so serious* about wanting to achieve financial freedom and generate passive income that I really started to make some changes that were *actually* working in my favor.

In just under two years, I got all my money back—and gained almost a *few times* the money I'd lost back. Now, I only work a few hours a week, thanks to the tools and AI trading systems I use. I make my monthly income being totally independent, doing what I want *when I want*. That's the real freedom we all want! I've experienced all stages of it. I started from scratch! So, I know all the mistakes that people make, and I know how to help you avoid them. Indeed, now my goal is to help other ambitious investors and traders achieve financial freedom and generate passive income, because the best thing you can do when you're good at something is to share it with others and make money at the same time. An important aspect of my journey? Learning how to take on **risk** in a *smart way*.

See, investment is all about putting your money *into something* in the hopes that once you take it out, more money will have been made in the process. Indeed, this is where the idea that 'You need to spend money to make money' comes from. If you want to make money, you have to be ready to spend it on something that will make you *more* money, because investments are about how we can *grow* what we already have. Throughout this chapter, we'll be having a look at the kinds of risks you need to be willing to deal with while investing in your future financial wealth. We'll be looking at how you can master risk and reward, including the strategies to follow to make informed and calculated investment decisions. Just to give you an idea, I invested $300K in 2010 that had turned into around $40M by 2024. That's the magic of long-term investment put in the right company. The Warren Buffet style! On that note, let's get started!

WHAT YOU NEED TO KNOW: UNDERSTANDING AND MANAGING RISKS IN INVESTING

One of the main reasons why people avoid going into fields such as the stock market is because they don't understand how it works. In other words, they aren't ready to take the risk of doing something that might not work out as planned, or that might not work out at all, because they're uninformed! Mastering risk and rewards is something you need to know how to do and become comfortable with if you truly want to create wealth for yourself. Wealth inevitably comes with some kind of risk, but that doesn't mean that the risk needs to be uncalculated. If you want to be a successful investor, you need to learn to navigate the shifting landscapes of financial markets.

Let's start with understanding and managing risks. The first step in mastering risk is understanding how diverse risk can be. Risk in investing isn't a one-size-fits-all! It has different forms. It varies a lot based on the asset class, market conditions, and investment strategies involved. For example, there's market risk, credit risk, liquidity risk, and operational risk, just to name a few. The type of risk we deal with requires us to use a specific approach to manage and mitigate it properly.

But effective risk management starts with *diversification*, which is what we're referring to when we say, 'Don't put all your eggs in one basket.' This is an old saying that simply refers to ensuring that you aren't placing all your bets on *one* singular investment, but instead, that you're *spreading* your risk over different kinds of investments. However, diversification isn't *just* about having a variety of investments; it's about **choosing assets** that respond differently to the same market events. For example, you'd want to have parts of your portfolio that can be used to reduce your overall volatility. So, if one of your investments were to turn out to be unprofitable, your other investments would be able to cover whatever loss you might be incurring. So, you're curbing overall volatility and reducing your risk of potential losses.

But diversification isn't the all-encompassing solution for your investment efforts. It has to be accompanied by a more thorough understanding of your risk tolerance and appetite, as well as your investment horizon. For example, a younger investor might tolerate *higher risks* for potentially *greater returns* because they have a longer time horizon. In other words, if they lose some money, it's not a big deal because they have more time ahead of them to prepare themselves for the worst, if something bad were to happen. On the other hand, someone who's getting close to retirement might not be willing to jeopardize their savings or investments, so they might prioritize safer investments. You need to know what *your* risk appetite is. How willing are you to take on risky investments? How willing are you to take on investments that might not work out perfectly in the long run? You need an investment strategy that fits your expectations and your willingness to take on more or less risk.

I always recommend adopting a risk–reward ratio in your trading, referring to the potential gain versus the potential loss of a trade. It's a crucial concept that you can use to assess the profitability and riskiness of your trades. A 3:1 risk–reward ratio, for example, means that for every unit of risk taken, you can expect to make three units of profit.

Let's consider an example to better understand this concept. Suppose you decide to buy a stock at $50 per share, with a stop-loss order set at $48 and a take-profit order at $56. In this scenario, you're risking $2 per share (the difference between the entry price and the stop-loss price) and aiming for a profit of $6 per share (the difference between the take-profit price and the entry price).

Let's break down the scenario:

1. **Entry point**: You initiate your position at **$50**.
2. **Stop-loss**: To limit potential losses, you set a stop-loss order at **$48**. If the stock price drops to or below this level, your position will be automatically sold to prevent further losses.
3. **Take-profit**: To secure profits, you set a take-profit order at **$56**. If the stock price reaches or exceeds this level, your position will be automatically sold, locking in gains.

In summary:

- **Entry point**: $50
- **Stop-loss**: $48
- **Take-profit**: $56

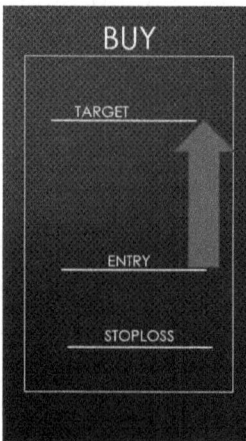

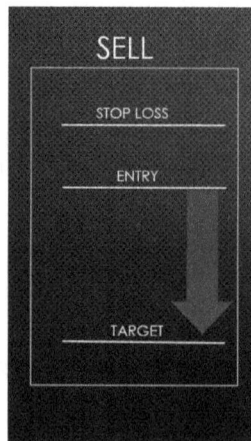

Remember, these levels are crucial for managing risk and maximizing returns in your stock trading strategy.

Now, when choosing a stock to invest in, it's important to conduct thorough research and analysis. Here are some key factors to consider:

1. **Company fundamentals**: Look into the company's financial health, earnings growth, revenue streams, and competitive positioning in the market.
2. **Industry trends**: Understand the industry the company operates in, including potential growth opportunities and any risks that may impact its performance.
3. **Market conditions**: Consider macroeconomic factors, market trends, and investor sentiment that could influence the stock's price.
4. **Technical analysis**: Analyze historical price movements, trading volumes, and patterns to identify potential entry and exit points.
5. **Big money flows**: Consider what the biggest investors are doing with their massive amounts of money.

That's the very reason behind the creation of Winning Wallet—to provide assistance to individuals seeking to invest in stocks and the real estate market. We invite you to connect with us for personalized, complimentary consultations where we can delve into potential opportunities together.

STRATEGIES FOR MAKING INFORMED AND CALCULATED INVESTMENT DECISIONS

I wish there was an easier option, but the bottom line of the strategy is that you need to **research** whatever decision you're planning on making. We live in a world that's constantly noisy—people might be yelling at you to invest in one scheme or another, but you might not be sure about what the right option is. So, this is where you need to be doing fundamental analysis, which is where you examine a company's financial statements and market position. You also analyze their technical analysis by focusing on patterns in market data. The goal is to gain a comprehensive understanding of the kind of decisions you're making, the impact they may have, and the information that's available for you to understand how risky that decision actually is. Of course, you'll also want to mix this with other strategies like macroeconomic overviews, while focusing on factors like interest rates, inflation, and geopolitical events.

You can also use a strategy that uses **stop-loss orders and position sizing**. Stop-loss orders are helpful in making sure you aren't losing more money by automatically selling an asset if it reaches a certain price. Position sizing, on the other hand, is based on the determination of how much of a particular asset to buy by balancing the potential profit against risk exposure.

Position sizing in trading the financial market refers to determining the amount of capital to invest in a particular trade based on various factors such as risk tolerance, account size, and market conditions. It involves calculating the appropriate number of shares or contracts to buy or sell to manage risk effectively.

For example, let's say you have a trading account with $10,000 and you're willing to risk 2% of your account on a single trade. If you're considering buying a stock priced at $50 per share, you'd calculate your position size as follows:

Risk per trade = 2% of $10,000 = $200

Stop-loss distance = $2 (assuming your stop-loss is set $2 below your entry price)

Position size = $200 / $2 = 100 shares

Therefore, in this example, you'd buy 100 shares of the stock priced at $50 per share to ensure you're not risking more than 2% of your account on that trade. Position sizing is a crucial aspect of risk management in trading to help protect your capital and maximize your potential returns.

Of course, throughout all this, you need to **stay updated and adaptable**. Remember, one of the pillars I follow throughout all areas of my life is ensuring that I'm continuously learning! This is applicable to many parts of my life, including making sure my strategies are in line with the market. After all, markets evolve, and so should your strategies! What worked yesterday might not work tomorrow, so you need to stay on top of all market trends if you truly want long-term success.

If you want to learn more, you can reach out to me on @serge.dfouni on Instagram.

Think about it this way. We're currently seeing high inflation across the board. This means that while your money is sitting in the bank and gaining interest, it might not even be making you money. It might, instead, be *costing you* money if the interest gained doesn't reach inflation levels. So, you need to diversify. You need to make sure you have various sources of income, and your money keeps making you more money all the time. Likewise, this is a good way to protect yourself against a potential economic crisis in the future. Indeed, investors who had much more spread-out investments in the 2008 crisis weren't as badly hurt as those who only had one form of investment. So, don't put all your eggs in the same basket.

Here are some examples of how you could diversify your investments in order to make your money work for you:

- Consider real estate investments for potential long-term growth.
- Short-term rental, known as Vacation Home Rental, is a great investment and requires small capital.
- Allocate funds to bonds or treasury securities for stability.
- Explore investing in commodities like gold or silver as a hedge against inflation.

- Invest in a diverse range of asset classes such as stocks, bonds, real estate, and commodities to spread risk and maximize returns.
- Consider investing in low-cost index funds or exchange-traded funds (ETFs) to gain exposure to a broad market without the need for active management.
- Explore alternative investments like cryptocurrency, mainly Bitcoin and Ethereum.

Ultimately, it all comes down to making decisions that *make sense*, and that requires a lot of research. If you're completely new to investing, you need to first educate yourself. You need to make sure you have the knowledge you need to make decisions that won't bankrupt you. So, if you know nothing about this field, start by learning the basics. Understand how the stock exchange works, the kind of stocks you can purchase and sell, when to buy, when to sell, and so on. You shouldn't be using the stock exchange and investing if you don't understand how it works, *generally speaking*. You need a solid baseline knowledge of how it all works, and *then* you can think about what else to do with it.

In my life, I've seen countless people fail financially because they invested in places or schemes that they shouldn't have invested in. They did so because they weren't educated on the topic. This is something I want you to avoid—so before you do anything, **make sure you know what you're getting yourself into!** Don't jump into investments if you don't understand them properly.

THE WARREN BUFFETT APPROACH

We can also learn a lot from the way Warren Buffett approaches investment fears, or rather guides individuals through them. The idea here is that you have to be able to overcome those fears—because unless you confront them head on, they can hold you back from managing your money and investments in a smart way.

According to Buffett, based on his book *Berkshire Hathaway Letters to Shareholders*,[1] whenever you're placing money in the stock market, you should do so with a long-term outlook. You need to be very comfortable with short-term losses so you can invest in your *long-term* gains, even if it means losing a bit at first. Likewise, Buffett says that there are two emotions we feel whenever we invest in the stock market: greed and fear. You need to be able to navigate those effectively.

But Buffett *also* thinks we have it the wrong way around whenever we try to manage our feelings when markets fluctuate. If you want to be a smart investor, do the opposite of what most investors are doing. So, for example, if everyone is talking about how great the stock market is doing, and whenever they're all talking about the incredible growth of their stocks and funds, you need to be extra-conscious of the actual state of the market because this may not be as accurate as you may think it is. Don't follow the crowd—your investment portfolio

---

1   https://www.goodreads.com/book/show/17972688-berkshire-hathaway-letters-to-shareholders

is *yours*, and it shouldn't be influenced by whatever others are saying. You need to have the final say.

However, if you hear people freaking out about the market being down, and whenever everyone's fears seem to be on high alert, it's time to buy! Buffett's thinking is that everything costs *less* in a down market. So, since we're in this for the long run, we're bound to make a profit in the long term!

IMPORTANT POINTS TO KEEP IN MIND

Once you're ready to start investing, you might start feeling extremely excited and over the moon about beginning this exciting new journey. However, make sure you keep a few things in mind. For example, the stock market *will* rise and fall. This is part of the deal—and it's also why we get so worried about investing in the first place! The market is completely unpredictable, despite our best attempts at predicting it. You might be a stock analyst, but you can't predict with perfect accuracy which stocks and funds will be successful or will completely fail. Likewise, you should **take your own situation into consideration**. For instance, if you're planning on retiring in five years, you might not have enough time to invest in aggressive growth stocks *and experience growth*—this might just not be long enough. On the other hand, if you've got fifteen to twenty more years, the aforementioned ideas and suggestions are likely to work for you.

A helpful way to lower your risk is also to diversify. You want to take on *different kinds* of stocks and investments to lower the amount of risk you're taking on.

I mentioned earlier what I believe are the best investment vehicles to grow your wealth. Below are examples of how you can diversify your investments in the stock market, based on different industries or segments:

1. **Technology**: Companies involved in technology, such as software development, hardware manufacturing, and internet services.
2. **Financial services**: Banks, insurance companies, and investment firms that provide financial services to individuals and businesses.
3. **Healthcare**: Companies involved in healthcare services, pharmaceuticals, biotechnology, and medical equipment manufacturing.
4. **Consumer goods**: Companies that produce and sell products for personal or household use, such as food and beverage companies, clothing retailers, and consumer electronics manufacturers.
5. **Energy**: Companies involved in the production and distribution of energy, including oil and gas producers, renewable energy firms, and utilities.
6. **Industrials**: Companies that manufacture industrial products, provide transportation services, or are involved in infrastructure development.

7. **Consumer services**: Companies that provide services to consumers, such as retail stores, restaurants, and travel companies.

These are just a few examples of the different industries within the stock market. Each industry has its own unique characteristics and can be influenced by different factors such as market trends, regulatory changes, and economic conditions. It's important for investors to diversify their portfolios across multiple industries to reduce risk and maximize potential returns.

This will also help you reduce the amount of stress you're under if your stocks aren't doing well. Speaking of which, make sure you don't let yourself get scared out of investing. Don't withdraw from great opportunities to invest—you're also withdrawing from the possibility to succeed in the long-term as well.

Here are a few more personal tips for this. Yes, you'll experience fears once in a while. Fear is normal! You're bound to be fearful once in a while; that's only part of life. Fear is *healthy* because it's telling you that something unsettling or worrying is happening. So, you need to rationalize that fear. You need to think about what it's trying to tell you, what you can take from it, and how you can use it to protect yourself. You can also reduce that fear by minimizing your risks through diversification. This means that you need to make some wise investments *in spite of* your fear. Look through all your investments and remember that as long as you have the right judgment, your money *will* grow. You can make one or two bigger investments when prices are down, but remember only to invest what you can afford to lose.

The more you get used to investing, the easier it will become, and the less stressful it will be.

CHAPTER 5

INVESTING IN YOURSELF AND YOUR FUTURE

*'THE BEST INVESTMENT YOU CAN MAKE IS
AN INVESTMENT IN YOURSELF ...
THE MORE YOU LEARN, THE MORE YOU'LL EARN.'*

—WARREN BUFFETT

This quote struck me many years ago; it was a source of inspiration that motivated me with the realization that the more I learn, the more I earn. From that moment, I developed the habit of reading daily about relevant subjects aligned with my dreams, whether it was investing, self-development, self-mastery, the mind, limiting beliefs, brain function, and so on. I sought out seminars that could expand my reach and connect me with like-minded people in my industry. I started investing in mentors and courses to become the best version of myself. I attended biohacking seminars to learn more about human potential. If you want to do better, you have to *be* better. Investing in yourself is a powerful way to enhance personal growth, gain the right knowledge you're missing, and achieve success.

Unfortunately, I realized a bit too late that I needed to get some help, as you saw in the previous chapter. But thankfully, I ended up meeting my business partner and mentor, a seasoned trading guru. Our partnership under the banner of Winning Wallet wasn't just a business alliance, but a journey of shared dreams and mutual growth, one we were incredibly proud to be going through together!

I started five years ago as a curious student under a senior's mentorship, who offered comprehensive courses and advanced software. I was incredibly immersed in learning, so I rapidly progressed from being a *newbie* to a proficient trader. But this wasn't a smooth road at all. Initially, I faced the same challenges as many traders—the emotional rollercoaster that often leads to significant losses. However, through my mentor's and business partner's guidance, I discovered the importance of *emotionless, systematic AI trading*. This approach, focusing on minimizing risk and maximizing profit, proved to be a game-changer.

Then, I became more and more successful at what I was doing, and so did my vision. So, my business partner and I decided to formalize our partnership. Our decision was driven by a shared ambition to reach and educate more people about financial literacy and the importance of informed trading decisions and real estate investments. So, the Winning Wallet venture was launched!

Winning Wallet emerged as the embodiment of our *collective* dream. The initiative goes beyond just teaching trading techniques; it's about empowering ordinary people with the knowledge and tools to achieve financial independence. I have a knack for marketing and community-building, focusing also on the real estate investment part, while my business partner, with his deep trading expertise, could create a synergy that turned Winning Wallet into a beacon of financial education.

EDUCATING YOURSELF: TOOLS AND RESOURCES

In the previous chapter, I mentioned how important educating yourself is to this process. If you want to really grow, and if you want to achieve your financial goals, you need to educate yourself on financial wellbeing. For this, you need to start by having the right goals. So, take some time now to think about what exactly you're trying to achieve. What are your financial goals? Why do you want to achieve them? As Tony Robbins says, 'Energy flows where attention goes.' To get what you really want in life, you need a clear goal that has purpose and meaning behind it.

Once you have your goals, start thinking about where you can find the resources and the solutions, or the tools, to get there. For example, investing in networking and building relationships with like-minded individuals has opened many doors and new opportunities for me. Attending conferences, joining professional communities, and utilizing social media platforms have helped me engage with others in my industry and build new income streams. If you want to make money, and if you want to be successful, look at the people around you who *have* that money and that fame. Look at how they're doing and how they got there. They have the answer to your question, or to your problem. They know how to make money and how to make it sustainably, so go and ask them about it. Invest in courses, coaching, and mentors. Surround yourself with individuals who inspire you and can offer guidance. Mentors can provide valuable insights, support, and accountability on your personal and professional growth journey, so they can be there for you whenever you have questions or aren't sure of the next few steps.

INVESTING IN YOURSELF: YOUR ROUTINES

To succeed, you can't just 'wing it'. **You need a plan**. You need to know exactly what you want to achieve, and how you'll achieve it. This can't be done by just 'winging it'—you have to plan out exactly how this will happen. I know I had to completely change my outlook on my own routine. I had to invest more time into creating a life that I wanted. So, have a look at the kind of routine you might want. What does it look like? How are you going to dedicate time every single day to improving yourself, improving who you are and what you do? How are you going to work every day towards reaching your financial goals? It all starts with the routines you have. Make sure you make time each day for your goals, whether that's time to read up on the current state of the economy, your investments, or a course teaching you how to create your very own passive income stream.

Likewise, you need to have excellent time management, and that was a big one for me! You need to put in the focus needed to complete the most important tasks. These have to be aligned with who you want to be and what you want to achieve in life. Be laser-focused on your goals and results! This is how you learn to prioritize tasks, minimize distractions, and maintain your focus on what *actually* matters, instead of focusing on all kinds of things that aren't important. Use tools if they help you—calendars, to-do lists, time-blocking—and find tools that will help you stay on track with your financial goals, like a budget planner.

You should also consider your weaker areas. Think about the areas you'd consider weaknesses. How can you invest more in each area? Which books, seminars, mentors, and so on can you learn from? Investing in yourself also means setting yourself up financially, but you can only achieve this if you have the baseline knowledge, which is why you need the routines. You need to know what you'll learn, what you *still* need to learn, when you'll learn it, and how it will apply to your goals to stay on track.

This also means that you might have some sacrifices to make. You might have to say no once in a while, even if it hurts. You might have to tell someone that unfortunately, you can't do this cool project, or go on this fun vacation, because you're currently working on building a life for yourself. You'll have to make sacrifices, but they'll all be worth it. You're investing in your future—you're bypassing fun *now* to set yourself up for a happy, fulfilling, and financially secure *future*, and that's invaluable.

THE KEY TO A FINANCIALLY SECURE FUTURE

Once you've got the routines down, you can start working towards your financially secure future. Lesson Number One is that you need to **learn how to use your money**. Most of us were never taught how to manage our finances. I had to change my mindset about money by starting to learn about financial education and investing, which was a turning point for me. We need to change our mindset to master our money and invest *wisely*.

Invest early, invest often. I've always believed that investing at an early stage in life sets you up for financial freedom. My advice is to start saving early with whatever you have. Change your mindset about spending money on shiny objects, clothes, watches, and cars. This is the wrong mentality. Instead, invest often in yourself, in new skills, in courses, in mentorships, in learning, in reading books, and in projects, businesses, stocks, bonds, trading, real estate, and side hustles so you have multiple sources of income.

Don't fall into the trap of pure saving. That's what banks want you to do. That's what they teach, and that's what the media does to us. They brainwash us to save our money in the banks and live in this illusion. We've been taught that since we were young, by our parents. And the ugly truth is that banks take your money and invest it in businesses, projects, bonds, stocks, real estate, etc., and make huge profits from your money. Meanwhile, your money loses value over time due to inflation and because you didn't employ it properly or invest it to grow and compound.

I invested in stocks a long time ago. I'd invest small amounts of money and watch it grow over time, which brought a lot of self-enjoyment. Although I lost some and won at other times, throughout the years, I learned the art of investing and got better as I grew older. I learned that investing should be viewed as a long-term project, with the power of compounding and multiplying over time.

Investing in collaborations and relationships with the right people, aligned with your vision, is crucial. Not with everyone, but only with those people who are aligned with your goals and where you want to be.

Let me illustrate this to you. When I was fifteen or sixteen, during big festivals in my city, I'd lease land that wasn't being used and turn it into a parking space. I enlisted some friends to assist me, helping people park their cars since it was getting crowded everywhere during the event. My job was to solve a problem for people, allowing them to enjoy the festival with their family. I used to make a lot of pocket money for my age, and that brought me a lot of joy and a sense of fulfillment and confidence in myself.

Then, when I turned seventeen, I worked for a few summers in the port, helping my uncle clear shipments for his clients and making some great money doing that. I had to get in with the grown-ups, learn the logistics world inside-out (including shipping and clearance), and be able to prove to myself and my family that I could do the job right. It was quite an experience where I acquired new skills and pushed myself to grow personally and professionally. I could grow my confidence, learn new things, and challenge myself to do more in the future.

What I did with the money wasn't just about spending. I helped my parents and spoiled my sister. I invested in courses and books. From the beginning, though, I had to learn to be smart about money, or I wouldn't have been able to grow it.

TOOLS TO SUCCEED

You need to start early and be consistent. Time is one of the most valuable assets in investing. The earlier you start investing, the more time your money has to grow through compounding returns. Consistently contribute to your investments, even if it's a small amount initially.

Suppose you'd invested $100 in Bitcoin in 2010 when the price was around $0.08 per coin. At that time, you would have acquired 1,250 BTC. Fast-forward to today, with the price of Bitcoin hovering around $50,000 per coin. That initial $100 investment would now be worth a staggering $62.5 million.

Now, let's look at another example of an investment in growing trendy stocks like artificial intelligence, electric cars, or technology companies.

If someone had invested $1,000 in Tesla (TSLA) stock back in 2010 when it was trading at around $20 per share and held onto it until now when the stock is valued at approximately now worth $220 per share (in the time I wrote this book, as price will always fluctuate), that initial investment would have grown to $40,000. This represents a significant growth driven by the rising popularity and success of electric cars.

Investing in innovative sectors like AI, electric cars, technology or any trending markets can offer substantial returns over time due to their potential for disruptive growth and market expansion.

Likewise, you need to adopt a long-term mindset. Investing isn't a get-rich-quick scheme. It requires patience and discipline. Avoid making impulsive decisions based on short-term market fluctuations and focus on your long-term goals. However, one extremely important point to highlight is to always invest in your current job or business first. Go all in, ensuring it's successful and provides enough for your future before you start investing in anything else. Investment should always come *after* you have a steady income stream from your current work or business. And always invest only what you can afford to lose.

Moreover, invest in your physical wellbeing, health, and vitality. Longevity can be both a goal and a decision. If you protect your mind and control your thoughts, care about the food you put in your body, and recognize how alcohol affects your brain, adopting a healthy lifestyle becomes crucial. Regular exercise, proper nutrition, and sufficient rest will definitely increase your chances of living much longer. Prioritizing your health by adopting a healthy lifestyle and maintaining high energy levels has a direct impact on your success, resilience, decision-making, and results in your life.

Finally, invest early, invest often, and invest in different ways.

Now, let's head to the next chapter where we discuss more about the investment types.

CHAPTER 6

PASSIVE VERSUS ACTIVE INVESTING

'I WOULD RATHER BE CERTAIN OF A GOOD RETURN THAN HOPEFUL OF A GREAT ONE.'

—WARREN BUFFETT

We've explored quite a few aspects involved in investing, but one aspect that we haven't touched on just yet is the difference between passive and active investments. You might have read about how *passive income* is crucial to establish real wealth, and that's true. You want your money to *make you more money.* In other words, you want to invest in activities, products, services, business ideas, and the like, that are likely to start making *you* more money by generating an income. Think of real estate, the stock market, and so on. Let's have a look at what all this entails.

ACTIVE INVESTING:
HIGHER RETURNS, BUT ...

There are different kinds of investors, namely **active** and **passive** investors. Each has their own benefits. However, they *also* have their downsides. Let's start with the **active investors**. Active investors are those who like to pick a specific investment product with the intention of making it yield a return that's higher than average. It's a great option if you want potentially higher returns, but it can *also* carry more risks. As an active investor, you most likely have your own system when it comes to selecting investments and creating a strategy that works *for you*.

You also usually **pick stocks**. That might include bonds or mutual funds if you think they might make you more money, but this isn't *always* the case. You namely look for stocks that you like and that you've evaluated as having a high potential for profit. This means that you probably also invest in the short term instead of the long term, because your main goal is to make *profits* right away. So, once you see that your investment's no longer likely to make you money—such as when the stock market becomes shaky—this is when you choose to pull out. It's a great way to earn a good return on your investment without taking on risk you aren't comfortable with.

You probably also choose exactly when you'll enter and exit a trade. For example, you might use stop-loss points to make sure you get rid of your investment before you lose too much money. This is your way of dealing with risk—you make sure you only take on what you know you can tolerate. This way, you also don't know how much you might lose in the long run, but this is something that *passive* investors tend to care more about.

In addition to investing in individual stocks, there are several other types of active investing strategies you can explore. Some popular options include:

1. **Bonds**: Investing in bonds involves loaning money to a company or government in exchange for regular interest payments and the return of the initial investment at a specified future date.
2. **Mutual funds**: These are investment vehicles that pool money from multiple investors to buy a diversified portfolio of stocks, bonds, or other securities managed by a professional fund manager.
3. **Exchange-traded funds (ETFs)**: Similar to mutual funds, ETFs also hold a basket of securities but trade on stock exchanges like individual stocks.
4. **Options and futures**: These are derivative securities that derive their value from an underlying asset, such as stocks, bonds, commodities, or currencies. They can be used for speculation or hedging purposes.
5. **Real estate**: Investing in real estate involves buying properties with the expectation of generating rental income and/or capital appreciation.
6. **Commodities**: This includes investing in physical goods like gold, silver, oil, or agricultural products, either directly or through commodity futures contracts.

Each type of active investing has its own risk–return profile and requires a different level of expertise and research. It's essential to understand the characteristics of each option before deciding which one aligns best with your investment goals and risk tolerance.

You probably also use **leverage**, which most active investors use to keep track of price fluctuations, take advantage of them, and again *maximize profits*. This way, you might earn a higher return than you would with your own capital. And finally, you use information that's *reliable and trustworthy* to make your decisions. Instead of following the crowds (which we discussed a few chapters ago), you only make financial decisions you believe are trustworthy based on the information you can find yourself and you find reliable. You don't listen to the fearmongering, and you're good at knowing when something is public panic, versus when it's truly worrying.

Let's dig more into what leverage means. Leverage trading involves borrowing funds to increase the size of your trading position, enabling you to potentially amplify profits (or losses) based on the price movements of the asset. Here are some common examples of leverage trading:

1. **Margin trading**: This is a popular form of leverage trading where traders borrow funds from a broker to buy or sell assets. By using margin, traders can control larger positions with a smaller amount of capital.

2. **Futures contracts**: Futures trading allows investors to speculate on the future price movements of an asset without owning the asset itself. Traders can use leverage to control a larger position in the futures market than they could with their own capital.

3. **Options trading**: Options contracts give traders the right, but *not* the obligation, to buy or sell an asset at a specified price before a certain date. By using options with leverage, traders can potentially earn higher returns on their investments.

4. **CFDs (Contracts for difference)**: CFDs are derivative products that allow traders to speculate on the price movements of various financial instruments without owning the underlying asset. Leverage is commonly used in CFD trading to magnify potential profits.

Let's look at an example of leverage so it makes more sense to you. Say you want to purchase a hundred shares of a stock priced at $50 per share. Without using margin, the total cost would be $5,000 (100 shares x $50). However, with a 10:1 margin, for example, you can control a position worth $50,000 by only putting up $5,000 of your own capital.

In this scenario, you borrow $45,000 from the broker to complete the purchase. If the stock price increases to $55 per share and you decide to sell, you'd make a profit of $500 ($55 sell price vs. $50 buy price) on each share, totaling $5,000 profit (100 shares x $5). After repaying the borrowed amount of $45,000 plus any interest or fees to the broker, you'd keep the remaining profit as your own.

This example illustrates how leverage trading can be utilized by active investors to capitalize on price fluctuations and potentially enhance their returns, provided they understand and manage the risks involved. Remember to always trade responsibly and consider your risk tolerance when using leverage in your investment strategies.

WHEN IS ACTIVE INVESTING ADVANTAGEOUS?

Being an active investor can sometimes come in handy, and it does have some advantages. However, it isn't for everyone! It's true that it can bring in significant profits, but this is only true if you know what you're doing. This is also a great approach to adopt if you want to learn more about the market, analyzing the market, how to read market fluctuations, how to assess risks, and so on. Therefore, if your goal is to learn more, this is a great option.

It's *also* possible to be an active investor without actually having to be the one with all the information. In other words, you can transfer the responsibility to someone else, such as by hiring an expert who invests your funds for you based on their own knowledge and experience.

But like anything else in life, active investing can also be disadvantageous. Yes, you *can* learn how to do it, but if you don't know the basics or how to do this without taking on more risk than you can actually afford to, you may end up losing a lot. Likewise, using leverage to get more returns can be very risky—and although I'm all about taking on more risk, you should never invest in something that you can't afford to lose! If the value of the investment product doesn't increase as you expect it to, you'll have to place *more* money into your account just to cover what you've lost. So, you aren't *just* losing your investment. You're losing much more money than you initially agreed to invest in the first place.

You'll also need to watch out for speculation, because as an active investor, you might make the mistake of putting too much trust into a single piece of information. **Don't** overpay for an investment just because of the wrong *perceived* value. Make sure that the value actually reflects the real value of the investment. Again, this comes down to experience and knowing how to read the market! This isn't something you can learn just through books; you have to *experience* it.

And even if information *were* available, it's not always great. Indeed, good information is often quite difficult to find. This means that it may be very challenging to find information to base your investment decisions on, and that you might be taking on more *stress* than you initially signed up for, just because you're not sure how to approach your investments.

So, all in all, active investing is very time-consuming! It can be extremely stressful too, because you're never 100% sure about your investments, and you're constantly looking out for what might happen that you haven't planned for, or what you might not be entirely ready to confront money-wise. It takes time to learn how to make the best decisions, and to create a strategy that works perfectly for you.

But if active investing is still your preferred strategy, don't hold back from trying it out with someone who's more experienced than you are. You can always consider actively managed funds! These might be on the more expensive side and might not be worth it because the fees might take away most of your investment, but they're worth considering nonetheless.

I consistently follow a structured method and dedicate myself to gaining knowledge in the realm of investing to minimize the risk of failure and maximize the potential for success. This is why I utilize an AI algorithm system that identifies investment opportunities in stocks, commodities, or ETFs, allowing me to make informed decisions at the right times and for the right prices. It's also very effective and works with the same efficiency for those interested in forex or cryptocurrencies.

I depend on a proven system that's been successful for over twenty years. This system utilizes AI, machine learning, and advanced algorithm programming to deliver accurate data with a 70% success rate.

If you want to know more about it, you can always reach out to me on my personal Instagram page at @serge.dfouni

PASSIVE INVESTORS: LONG-TERM PERSPECTIVE

On the other end of the spectrum, we have *passive investors*. These are the kind of investors that Warren Buffett talks about (as we saw in the previous chapters). Passive investors might yield more average but **steady** returns. They look at the bigger market, seeking *long-term* investments instead of short-term investments. You might be a passive investor if you're looking to invest to build your retirement, for example.

Passive investment strategies are different from active ones. They're focused on *low volatility*, meaning that they're more stable and grow over time, instead of fluctuating a lot, making you unsure of whether your investment will continue to make you money tomorrow, or whether it will cost you down the line. These might be, for example, index funds, ETFs (Exchange-Traded Funds), or individual stocks.

As a passive investor, you're also creating a diversified portfolio to make sure that at least *one* of the sectors you're exposed to will lead to a profit. Again, this shows you the goal: To make average but *steady* returns instead of earning as much as possible. The plus side? You're making a much steadier investment, and therefore, you're taking on a lot less risk than you would with other forms of investments.

You also look at *historical data* to make your decisions, as well as the current market. Unlike active investors, you don't make decisions solely on the basis of what you think might work out well *now* considering the current market. You look at the *bigger picture*. You look at the historical aspect—how has the stock changed over time? What kind of trends have you witnessed? Do you think this is likely to change in the future? This is the kind of information you pay attention to, because you aren't only interested in investing in what makes sense right now, but especially in what makes sense to invest in *for the long term*.

This is directly related to the amount of risk appetite that you have. You might be willing to take on more risk if it means greater returns. Or, you might be willing to take on less risk but wait a longer period of time to see your investment working. This is down to the kind of risk-taker that you are, and whether you'd like to see *immediate* returns or whether you can afford to wait a few years (for example, if you're saving for retirement).

Here are some examples of passive investment types:

1. **Index funds**: Index funds are a type of mutual fund or exchange-traded fund (ETF) that aims to replicate the performance of a specific market index, such as the S&P 500. By investing in an index fund, you can gain exposure to a broad range of stocks or bonds without having to actively manage your investments.
2. **ETFs**: ETFs are similar to index funds, but trade on an exchange like a stock. They offer investors a way to invest in a diversified portfolio of assets at a low cost. Examples of popular ETFs include the SPDR S&P 500 ETF (SPY) and the Vanguard Total Stock Market ETF (VTI).

3. **Individual stocks**: While individual stocks aren't typically considered passive investments, you can still take a passive approach by investing in blue-chip companies with a long track record of success. For example, companies like Apple, Microsoft, Meta, Amazon, Google, and Johnson & Johnson are often seen as stable long-term investments that can provide steady returns over time.

In summary:

1. Index funds:
   - provide broad market exposure by tracking a specific index.
   - are passively managed with low expense ratios.
   - offer diversification across various sectors and industries.
2. ETFs (Exchange-Traded Funds):
   - trade on stock exchanges like individual stocks.
   - can track various indices, sectors, or commodities.
   - provide flexibility for intraday trading and diversification.
3. Individual stocks:
   - involve direct ownership in a specific company.
   - offer potential for higher returns but also higher risk.
   - requires active monitoring and research compared to index funds or ETFs.

Moreover, here are some potential passive investment types for index funds, ETFs, and individual stocks to look into:

1. **Broad market index funds**: These funds track the performance of an entire market, such as the S&P 500 or the total stock market index.
2. **Sector-specific ETFs**: These funds focus on specific sectors of the economy, such as technology, healthcare, or energy.
3. **Dividend-paying stocks**: Investing in individual stocks of companies that pay dividends can provide a steady stream of income over time.
4. **Bond index funds**: These funds invest in a diversified portfolio of bonds, providing a relatively stable source of income.
5. **International index funds**: Investing in funds that track international markets can help diversify your portfolio and potentially reduce risk.
6. **Real estate investment trusts (REITs)**: REITs are a type of security that invests in real estate properties and can provide investors with regular income streams.
7. **Growth stocks**: Investing in individual stocks of companies with strong growth potential can offer the opportunity for significant capital appreciation over time.
8. **Value stocks**: These are stocks considered undervalued by the market and may offer potential for long-term growth as their value is recognized.

I also have a new solid program launched a few years ago that's completely passive, which I spoke about in previous chapters. If you'd like to know more about it, you can always reach out to me personally on @serge.dfouni

WHAT BENEFITS ARE THERE TO PASSIVE INVESTING?

Just like active investing, there are benefits and disadvantages to take into consideration with passive investing. Indeed, you'll be able to enjoy lower risks and fees, because less 'work' needs to be done. Most of the work is done once you have your initial investments set up—it only becomes a matter of making sure that your investments are relatively stable. This consistency is also seen in your profits—they're consistent too, not volatile like those you see in active investing. If you aren't risk-hungry, this is perhaps a better investing option for you.

But of course, this also means that you're not making the high returns that you may have thought you'd make initially. In fact, sometimes, returns are below average. On top of this, it can take a lot of time to build, because building a portfolio that touches on the right number and variety of sectors and assets can take a lot of a) time and b) capital. This isn't the same kind of investment as active—it's something that you really do over **time**.

SO, WHAT'S BEST FOR ME?

The big question: What kind of investor are you? This depends on different factors. For example, how much risk are you willing to take on? If you're the kind of person to constantly check your investments to make sure that you're not losing money, passive investment might be a good way to lower your stress. On the other hand, if you're the kind of person who prefers being in the heat of the action, and always trying to go one step further with your money, then you may benefit a lot more from being an *active* investor. Likewise, think about how much time you have to invest and reap the returns. Do what works *for you* based on real information, instead of doing what someone else tells you to do. **You know the amount of risk you're willing to take on**. If you aren't sure, follow the 1-to-3 ratio, which is that for every dollar risked, there should be a three-dollar potential profit or reward.

CHAPTER 7

UNLOCKING THE POTENTIAL OF REAL ESTATE INVESTMENTS

'NINETY PERCENT OF ALL MILLIONAIRES BECOME SO THROUGH OWNING REAL ESTATE. MORE MONEY HAS BEEN MADE IN REAL ESTATE THAN IN ALL INDUSTRIAL INVESTMENTS COMBINED.'

—ANDREW CARNEGIE,
BILLIONAIRE INDUSTRIALIST

From humble beginnings to achieving financial independence, I've learned firsthand the importance of mindset,
strategy, and perseverance in unlocking the wealth-building
potential of real estate. If you haven't invested in real estate,
now is the time. Shift your perspective and adopt the real
estate investor mindset. Real estate is an investment vehicle
where your money works for you, generating active or passive income and wealth accumulation without the constraints
of traditional employment. This vision of financial freedom
is not merely a pipedream but a tangible reality achievable
through strategic investment in real assets.

Real estate investing embraces the concept of passive income
exceeding earned income, a paradigm shift that empowers
you to break free from the limitations of conventional employment. By investing in income-generating tangible assets, individuals can create streams of income that provide financial
security and freedom.

But what sets real estate apart as the ultimate wealth-building vehicle? Real estate offers a unique blend of benefits,
including cash flow, tax advantages, inflation hedging, and
refinance potential. Unlike liabilities such as cars and luxury
items that drain resources and depreciate in value, tangible
assets like rental properties appreciate over time and produce
steady income streams.

Historical return on investment (ROI) numbers for real estate
investments can vary significantly depending on factors such
as location, property type, market conditions, and investment

strategy. However, some general trends and historical averages provide insight into the performance of real estate as an asset class over time. Here are a few:

- **Long-term appreciation**: Real estate has historically exhibited long-term appreciation, with property values increasing over time. According to data from the Case-Shiller Home Price Index, which tracks home prices in the United States, the average annualized home price appreciation rate has been around 3–5% over the long term.
- **Rental income**: Rental income from investment properties is another significant component of ROI for real estate investors. The rental yield, or the annual rental income as a percentage of the property's value, can vary depending on factors such as location, property type, and market conditions. In the United States, the average gross rental yield for residential properties is typically in the range of 7–10%, although this can vary widely by market.
- **Cashflow**: Cashflow is the net income generated by a rental property after accounting for expenses such as mortgage payments, property taxes, insurance, maintenance, and vacancy costs. Positive cash flow is a key indicator of a successful rental property investment, providing ongoing income for investors.
- **Leverage**: One of the advantages of real estate investing is the ability to use leverage, or borrowed funds, to amplify returns. By financing a portion of the property purchase with a mortgage, investors can increase their

potential ROI by using other people's money to acquire and control assets.

- **Tax benefits**: Real estate investors also benefit from various tax advantages, including deductions for mortgage interest, property taxes, depreciation, and expenses related to property management and maintenance. These tax benefits can enhance the overall ROI of real estate investments by reducing the investor's taxable income and increasing cash flow.

Real estate investing involves risks, including market fluctuations, economic downturns, tenant turnover, and unforeseen expenses, which can impact overall returns. However, real estate is a tangible asset and one of the most stable and consistent investments historically. It comes down to shifting your mindset to a diversified and long-term investment strategy and learning about real estate as an investment.

REAL ESTATE INVESTMENT
Factors for Real Estate Investing

REAL ESTATE INVESTMENT

UNDERSTANDING THE
REAL ESTATE MARKET

Real estate is a world of its own, and there are concepts that you should understand before investing. Given the different ways you can invest in real estate, market trends and cycles, and picking the right investment, it might seem a little overwhelming. However, once you enter the arena, there's an abundance of information and people who are willing to help.

The first thing to know is that real estate can be an active or passive investment. For example, you might decide to buy residential properties and fix them up, then resell them or rent them out. As an active investor, you'd view the properties, maybe even do some renovations yourself, and then decide to manage the property without a property management company. Conversely, you might decide you don't want to be hands-on, so you buy a percentage of an apartment complex through a silent partnership or buy REITs through your stock portfolio. There's no right or wrong answer, but you must decide whether to invest in active or passive assets—or both.

Once you decide on an active or passive investment, you should understand the market for that investment. Like other investments, real estate has trends, cycles, and economic indicators that affect the market. The difference is that real estate has macro and micro trends based on the overall US market and the market where the property is physically located. Prices and real estate appreciation can be impacted positively or negatively from many different directions.

When looking at overall economic conditions, things like interest rates or an unexpected upheaval like the pandemic can negatively impact prices, appreciation, sales, and activity. However, just like the stock market, often it's when people panic that you find opportunity. Real estate investors often buy property during uncertainty because real estate is tangible. They know they'll physically own an asset that will eventually provide returns. The cycle is predictable.

When looking at a micro level for residential real estate, appreciation, sales, and prices could change due to the local economy, such as unemployment or development. For example, if a large company decides to leave the area and people can't find work, you might see an increase in homes for sale, creating pressure on prices. Conversely, if a new work center is developed in the area, this could attract workers and create pressure on inventory, leading to higher prices due to low inventory.

Local seasons can also have an impact on residential real estate markets. For example, many areas see peak selling season in the spring and early summer. On the other hand, property prices often decline slightly when selling at the end of the year into the new year. People don't want to move during the holidays and cold weather. As a savvy investor, you want to buy when prices are suppressed. Often, those trying to sell at the end of the year have no choice.

When it comes to commercial real estate or multifamily residential, the market conditions, trends, and impacts can differ slightly, but most of the same trends still follow. For example, if a local government offers large corporate incentives to buy or build there, you may see an uptick in commercial building and activity. The cost of land could go up. Multifamily housing will follow the work centers and local economies. For example, if the cost of living is too high, affordable apartments might be built compared to large single-family homes.

Because of the vast differences in local economies, it's wise to do due diligence in the area of interest before jumping in and buying property. You need to know how the local economy will impact your investments.

Finally, if you decide to invest passively by buying REITs or joining a syndication, you must still research the investment. Like personally owning tangible property, REITs and syndications own tangible property that can be impacted by all the above factors. You can't avoid doing the research. However, once you've done the research, you can begin to build an investment strategy.

BUILDING A REAL ESTATE INVESTMENT STRATEGY

Your investment strategy is often as unique as your fingerprint. This is because everyone must consider factors such as risk tolerance, investment objectives, and market dynamics. Each investment avenue comes with its own set of benefits and challenges, requiring thorough due diligence and a strategic approach to maximize returns and mitigate risks. Therefore, building wealth through real estate investments requires a tailored approach that aligns with your financial goals, risk tolerance, and investment preferences. Whether you're seeking passive income, long-term appreciation, or portfolio diversification, crafting a personalized wealth-building strategy is essential for success.

Understanding Your Investment Objectives

Before diving into the world of real estate investing, it's essential to clarify your investment objectives. Are you seeking passive income to supplement your existing income? Are you aiming for long-term appreciation to build wealth over time? Or perhaps you're looking to diversify your portfolio and mitigate risk through real estate investments? What are your limitations?

By identifying your investment objectives upfront, you can align your investment strategy with your financial goals and priorities. This clarity will guide your decision-making process and ensure that your investments align with your long-term vision for financial success.

Next, I previously mentioned active versus passive investing. Active investments require hands-on involvement in the day-to-day operations of properties, such as property management, renovation projects, and tenant relations. On the other hand, passive investments involve minimal involvement and typically entail investing in managed funds or properties where others handle the operational aspects. If you have the time and skills, active investing might interest you. However, if you lack the time and skills, consider passive investing. Let's explore the different types of real estate investments, considering both active and passive, as well as the pros and cons of each.

Types of Real Estate Investments

From stock portfolio REITs and syndications to residential rentals and land, each property type has its own set of benefits and challenges, requiring careful consideration based on investment objectives and market conditions. Take a look at the most notable:

- **Real estate investment trusts (REITs)**: REITs are publicly traded companies that own and manage income-producing real estate properties. This is a passive investment option with liquidity and diversification benefits. The good news is there's ease of entry. However, you have limited control and market dependency.
- **Wholesaling**: This is an active investment that involves finding off-market properties, securing contracts to purchase them at below-market prices, and assigning or flipping these contracts to end buyers. As an active investment, this requires negotiation skills and market knowledge. However, low initial capital is needed, and quick profits are often achieved. The negative is that this type of investing requires marketing and networking skills and has limited scalability.
- **Syndications**: This is a group of investors who pool funds from multiple investments to acquire larger commercial properties. Often, the investments are apartment buildings or complexes. This can be an active or passive investment. Passively, you can silently invest money, the properties are professionally managed, and the structured syndication group accounts for your return. Actively, you could be involved in daily operations, property management, or syndication activities through a skilled or elected position. This type of investment allows access to larger deals, diversification, and professional management. The

problem is you have limited control, and syndications are illiquid.

- **Fix and flip**: This investment is similar to wholesaling but involves purchasing distressed properties, renovating them, and selling them for a profit. It's an active investment, because even if you aren't doing the physical labor, you still have to acquire the properties and manage the renovations and sales. You need to have market knowledge or hire someone who does, as well as understanding the renovation process, including costs. The upside is the potential for high returns, and it gives you a creative outlet if you like interior design and renovation. However, this is a high-risk investment that's capital-intensive and time-consuming.

- **Commercial real estate**: Commercial real estate investment involves acquiring, owning, and operating income-generating properties used for business purposes rather than residential ones. These properties can include office buildings, retail centers, industrial warehouses, multifamily apartment buildings with five or more units, hotels, and mixed-use developments. Commercial properties typically generate higher rental income than residential properties due to longer lease terms and higher rental rates per square foot. They often have longer terms, ranging from three to ten years or more, providing stable and predictable cashflow for investors. Tenants are usually more stable and reliable compared to residential tenants. Unlike residential property leases, commercial tenants are often responsible for paying operating expenses such as property taxes, insurance, maintenance costs, and rent, reducing the landlord's expenses and management responsibilities. The upside is commercial properties have the potential for appreciation in value over time, driven by factors such as market demand, location, and property improvements. They also allow investors to diversify their portfolios beyond traditional asset classes like stocks and bonds, reducing overall investment risk. The issue is that commercial properties typically require a more significant upfront investment than residential properties due to higher purchase prices and additional financing requirements. Also, you may experience more extended vacancy periods between tenants, especially in economic downturns or during market fluctuations, leading to potential income loss. The complexity of ownership should also be considered because finding new tenants can be more challenging and time-consuming, and there's higher market risk due to industry-specific factors and regulatory considerations.

- **Land**: A land investment involves purchasing undeveloped or vacant land with the intention of holding it for future appreciation, development, or income generation. Land investments can range from small residential lots to large agricultural, commercial, or industrial parcels. The great news is the potential for appreciation: It's a low-cost and low-maintenance tangible asset to diversify your portfolio. You can develop the land, and this investment has tax benefits. However, vacant land generally doesn't produce income, is illiquid and speculative in nature, comes with market risk, and has holding costs.

- **Short- or long-term rentals**: Owning rental investments can be either passive or active depending on your level of property management. Short-term rentals can be more labor- and management-intensive and have high turnover. However, unlike long-term rentals, you often deal with less wear and tear since you maintain the property after every visitor. With both short and long-term rentals, you have the potential for consistent cashflow and tax benefits. However, you should expect operational challenges and regulatory considerations. Many places are now restricting short-term rentals; with long-term rentals, you risk tenants damaging the property or failing to pay rent.

Here, it's beneficial to explore rentals (specifically short-term rentals) in more depth. They're in a category of their own, with differing dynamics than traditional rental investments.

THE LURE OF SHORT-TERM RENTAL INVESTMENTS

The idea of short-term rentals as an investment is fairly new, but has become mainstream with platforms like Airbnb, VRBO, Booking.com, and others. However, the secret is out—if you have a rental property, short-term renting is lucrative due to the rise in tourism and holiday and business travelers' preferences for unique and personalized experiences beyond the traditional hotel stay.

Benefits of Short-term Rental Investments

Short-term renting or letting is typically for stays as short as one night and up to six months depending on your locality and any rules or restrictions regarding short-term rentals. These rentals are popular because they benefit guests and landlords or owners in several ways.

Benefits for guests include:

- Short-term letting offers business or leisure guests a low-cost alternative by staying in short-term property if the stay is more than a fortnight compared to hotels.
- The properties are well-maintained by either the host or a management company, providing additional amenities that offer the feel of a 'home away from home' to those occupying the property. They're typically booked fully furnished and equipped to accommodate guests with kitchens, living spaces, Wi-Fi, TV, toiletries and more.
- A greater degree of flexibility is offered when traveling for a number of weeks, or when moving to a new destination with the intention of permanent relocation. Potential guests have more freedom in this regard because they can stay and fully immerse themselves in a new location without making a long-term commitment.

Benefits to the owner and landlord include:

- Flexibility when selling the property due to the unpredictable nature of the selling process. Short-term letting allows the owner or seller the opportunity to continue profiting rather than leaving a property vacant like a traditional rental.

- More control over financial positions during economic shifts by avoiding long-term tenants. With long-term tenants, landlords have to time a sale with the end of the lease.
- With such a high demand for short-term lets in prime cities such as Dubai, landlords don't have to worry about dealing with difficult tenants and can be selective about whom they lease to. Most property management companies carry out a thorough vetting process to choose high-quality guests and will monitor and maintain the property throughout the process.
- Owning a short-term rental allows the freedom to block out certain dates for personal stays.
- Smart pricing technology and a well-experienced real estate agency to manage the property means you can adjust prices in accordance with market and seasonal demand. As a result, you can increase your price to maximize your earning potential rather than be held to a static price of a long-term lease.

Clearly, short-term rentals and vacation homes are an attractive investment option. You have the potential for greater cashflow, dynamic pricing, and more flexibility in managing the property. However, there are factors you must consider beyond the typical real estate rental.

Short-term Rental Considerations for Investors

Many of the same considerations will apply to short-term rentals as long-term rentals. From location to local regulations and amenities, investors must do their due diligence to ensure they're making a good financial decision. Here are a few things to consider:

- **Location**: Vacation or short-term rentals should be close to local tourist attractions, major work centers, amenities, and transportation hubs like airports. The first rule of real estate investing is *Location, Location, Location*. The only time you'd consider being off the beaten path is for guests that come to the area specifically to get away.
- **Guest preferences**: Consider the property size, layout, distinctive features, amenities, and design aesthetics of your guest. For example, if your area's known for young and vibrant nightlife, dining, and luxury, ensure you pick a property that will attract this type of guest. However, if the area's a destination for retired or older guests, consider properties with fewer stairs and amenities for this type of guest.
- **Create a memorable experience**: Guests want the ultimate experience. From interior design, furnishings, and comfort to convenience, you must go above and beyond the typical hotel stay. Consider things like keyless entry, complimentary toiletries, high-speed internet and Wi-Fi, local guidebooks, and personal recommendations for dining, shopping, and entertainment.
- **Management**: Short-term rentals require more hands-on management with cleaning and maintenance after

every guest. Will you manage the property, or will you hire someone? Fresh linens, toiletries, etc. will need to be replenished.

- **Furnishing and interior design**: To help elevate your rental so that it's memorable, be thoughtful in the interior design of spaces. Furniture should be durable but comfortable. Offer small appliances like hairdryers, coffee and teapots, as well as dishes and utensils. Consider soaps and lotions for bathrooms. Finally, consider a themed design so that you stand out among the competition.

- **Legal or regulatory restrictions**: Many areas are now regulating short-term rentals. Ensure you research and understand any zoning, licensing, tax, and homeowner association rules that could limit your investment potential.

One of the key attractions of investing in short-term vacation rentals is the potential for strong cashflow. By renting out your property on a nightly basis, you can generate higher rental income compared to traditional long-term leases. With careful pricing strategies and effective marketing, you can maximize occupancy rates and ensure a steady stream of income from your investment.

By exploring the diverse range of real estate investment options and assessing the associated risks, rewards, and limitations, you can build a resilient and diversified portfolio that lays the foundation for wealth accumulation and financial freedom. Of course, which investment you choose could be limited by your financing or seed money. So, let's look at how to finance your real estate investments before deciding on the type of investment to make.

FINANCING YOUR REAL ESTATE INVESTMENTS

When real estate investors take out loans to purchase real estate, it's called leverage. Using leverage, or borrowed funds, to finance real estate acquisitions can amplify returns and accelerate wealth accumulation, but it also comes with risks. Here are the pros of leverage:

- **Smaller initial investment**: Leverage allows investors to acquire properties with a smaller initial investment, enabling them to purchase more properties and diversify their portfolios, potentially turning into good debt.
- **Amplify returns**: By using leverage, investors can amplify the returns on their invested capital, as any appreciation in the property's value is magnified by the borrowed funds, potentially turning into good debt.
- **Preserved liquidity**: Leveraged financing preserves investors' liquidity by allowing them to retain more of their capital for other investment opportunities or unforeseen expenses, potentially turning into good debt.

But what's the downside? Consider the following:

- **Increased risk**: Using leverage increases the risk of financial loss, as investors are exposed to the potential for negative equity if the property's value decreases or rental income fails to cover mortgage payments, potentially turning into bad debt.

- **Higher financing costs**: Borrowing funds comes with costs such as interest payments, loan origination fees, and closing costs, which can reduce overall returns on investment, potentially turning into bad debt.
- **Cashflow vulnerability**: Leveraged properties may have higher mortgage payments, reducing cashflow and increasing vulnerability to fluctuations in rental income or unexpected expenses, potentially turning into bad debt.

Real estate investors can access various financing options to fund their property acquisitions, but not all debt is equal. Let's delve into the different financing options and discuss how they fit into the framework of leverage as good debt or bad debt.

Good Debt vs. Bad Debt

Understanding the difference between good and bad debts is essential for sound financial decision-making. While leveraging debt to acquire income-producing properties can enhance returns and amplify cashflow, avoiding excessive leverage and maintaining sufficient liquidity to weather market downturns and unforeseen expenses is crucial.

But what distinguishes good debts from bad debts in real estate investing? It all comes down to the underlying asset's ability to generate returns and appreciation over time. Borrowing money to invest in income-producing properties aligns with the principles of investing in assets that yield positive cashflow and long-term growth potential.

Conversely, bad debt is overleveraging your position in real estate or taking on risky debt with little return. For example, you want to purchase a property at the height of the market and offer over the asking price. You can't get traditional financing, so you agree to a high-interest-rate loan with unfavorable terms. The property needs work, so you put all the renovations on a credit card, intending to pay the card off when you sell the property. This nontraditional loan and credit card debt could be considered bad debt. The risks are high, and the entire investment is surrounded by uncertainty.

Let's explore the types of financing to get a better idea of good versus bad debt.

Types of Financing

In the real estate investment world, conventional mortgages are traditional loans that banks and lenders offer to purchase investment properties. These loans are considered good debt. Each lender or bank has an overarching set of lending rules and criteria an investor must meet to qualify for the loan. These requirements can include a minimum credit score, income and asset verification, and a certain percentage of the purchase price as a down payment. Other requirements might be projected revenue from the property, maintenance costs, vacancy rates, etc. These are general requirements. Then, there are lender overlays.

A lender overlay refers to additional guidelines or require-ments imposed by a mortgage lender that go beyond the min-imum standards set by government-sponsored enterprises (GSEs) such as Fannie Mae, Freddie Mac, or the Federal Housing Administration (FHA). These overlays are specific to individual lenders and are implemented to manage risk and ensure that loans meet the lender's internal criteria for approval.

Lender overlays typically address credit scores, debt-to-income ratios, down payment requirements, property types, and borrower qualifications. For example, while a GSE may accept a certain credit score for loan approval, a lender may impose a higher minimum credit score as part of their over-lay criteria to reduce the risk of default.

Lender overlays can vary widely from one lender to another and may change over time in response to market conditions, regulatory changes, or shifts in the lender's risk appetite. Borrowers seeking a mortgage loan should be aware of the specific overlay requirements of each lender and work closely with their mortgage advisor to understand how these over-lays may impact their ability to qualify for a loan.

It's good to know the general guidelines and then check with your preferred lender for any additional overlays. You may qualify for a loan with one lender but not another. For this reason, a savvy investor will shop around for lenders.

Of course, if you can't get a traditional loan, there are other options. The first is through private lending.

Bottom of form lenders are often called 'hard money lenders'. A hard money or private lender is an investor who provides short-term loans secured by real estate. These loans are typically used by real estate investors or developers who need financing quickly or may not qualify for traditional bank loans due to poor credit history, incomplete financial documentation, or the need for flexible lending terms.

Hard money loans are asset-based loans secured by the value of the underlying real estate property rather than the borrower's creditworthiness or income. The loan amount is typically based on the property's appraised value, and the lender may require a down payment or equity stake from the borrower to mitigate risk.

Private lenders usually charge higher interest rates and fees compared to traditional lenders, reflecting the increased risk associated with these loans and the short-term nature of the financing. The terms of hard money loans can vary widely depending on the lender and the specific circumstances of the transaction. Still, they often feature shorter repayment terms (e.g. six to twelve months) and may include balloon or interest-only payments.

Despite the higher costs and shorter terms, hard money loans can be a valuable financing option for real estate investors who need quick access to capital or may not qualify for traditional financing. These loans are commonly used for fix-and-flip projects, property renovations, bridge financing, or other short-term real estate investments where speed and flexibility are essential. However, borrowers should carefully evaluate the terms and costs of hard money loans and consider the potential risks before entering into any financing agreement. This good debt could quickly turn bad.

Other creative financing options exist, such as seller financing, lease options, and crowdfunding, which offer alternative ways to acquire properties with little or no money down. Creative financing can be a valuable tool for investors when employed strategically to secure favorable terms and minimize risk. However, investors should be wary of high-risk strategies that could lead to bad debt if the terms are unfavorable or unsustainable.

So, how can you ensure you leverage your investment with good debt without succumbing to bad debt? Let's take a look.

Tips for Securing Financing

Securing financing for investment properties requires careful planning, preparation, and negotiation, intending to acquire good rather than bad debt. Here are some tips to help investors improve their chances of securing favorable financing terms:

- **Improve credit scores**: Maintaining a high credit score is crucial for qualifying for favorable financing terms. Paying bills on time, reducing debt, and monitoring credit reports for inaccuracies can help improve credit scores over time.
- **Build relationships with lenders**: Establishing relationships with lenders and mortgage brokers can provide access to a broader range of financing options and increase the likelihood of securing favorable terms.
- **Prepare a strong loan application**: Prepare a comprehensive loan application package, including financial statements, tax returns, property appraisals, and a detailed investment plan, to demonstrate creditworthiness and the viability of the investment opportunity.
- **Negotiate favorable terms**: Negotiate with lenders to secure favorable terms such as lower interest rates, reduced fees, and flexible repayment options. Comparing offers from multiple lenders can help investors identify the most competitive financing options.
- **Consider alternative financing sources**: Explore alternative financing sources such as private lenders, crowdfunding platforms, and seller financing to access flexible financing options and potentially lower costs while carefully evaluating the terms to ensure they align with your investment objectives and risk tolerance.

Financing is a critical component of real estate investing, enabling investors to acquire properties, leverage their capital, and achieve their financial goals. By understanding the various financing options available, distinguishing between good and bad debt, and following essential tips for securing financing, investors can confidently make informed decisions and navigate the financing process. Remember to conduct thorough due diligence, seek professional advice when needed, and negotiate favorable terms to maximize returns and mitigate risks.

Once you secure financing, you can determine what real estate investment you want and search for opportunities.

FINDING AND EVALUATING INVESTMENT PROPERTIES

The first step in finding investment properties is identifying potential opportunities through various channels. To find properties listed for sale by owners, agents, or banks, you can start with real estate listings by browsing online platforms, such as multiple listing services (MLS), real estate websites, and property auctions. However, one underutilized resource is having a real estate network. Build relationships with real estate agents, wholesalers, investors, and other industry professionals who can provide leads on off-market properties or exclusive investment opportunities.

You could also use direct marketing and implement marketing strategies, such as direct mail campaigns, bandit signs (signs plastered over the neighborhood), and targeted online advertising, to attract property owners interested in selling their properties. Finally, consider joining a local real estate investment club to connect with like-minded investors, share knowledge and resources, and access potential investment opportunities.

No matter what you choose to implement, be sure you have criteria for selecting properties. Consider the following to ensure the property aligns with your investment objectives and financial goals:

- **Location**: Real estate values depend on *Location, Location, Location.* Choose properties in desirable neighborhoods with strong market fundamentals, such as high demand, low vacancy rates, good schools, amenities, and proximity to employment centers and transportation hubs.
- **Market demand**: Assess market conditions and trends, such as population growth, job growth, economic stability, and local development projects, to gauge demand for rental properties or potential for appreciation.
- **Financing options**: Consider the availability of financing options, such as conventional mortgages, hard money loans, or seller financing, and assess the impact of financing costs on the overall profitability of the investment.

Once you find a property that has potential, you must physically inspect the property to identify any potential issues or defects that may affect the property's value or investment potential. Hire qualified inspectors to assess the property's structural integrity, mechanical systems, plumbing, electrical, and other critical components. Review inspection reports carefully and factor any repair or maintenance costs into your investment analysis. Unexpected repair costs could turn a good debt bad very quickly.

Inspect and analyze the property's financials to determine its suitability as an investment. Calculate key financial metrics, such as cashflow, cap rate, gross rent multiplier (GRM), and return on investment (ROI), to assess the property's income-generating potential and compare it to other investment opportunities. Consider factors such as vacancy rates, rental market trends, property appreciation potential, and tax implications when evaluating the property's financial performance.

Finally, negotiate purchase agreements with sellers or their representatives to secure favorable terms and conditions for the investment property. Conduct market research to determine fair market value and leverage this information to negotiate prices, terms, and contingencies that protect your interests as an investor. Work closely with real estate agents, attorneys, and other professionals to navigate the negotiation process and ensure a smooth transaction from contract to closing.

Finding and evaluating investment properties is critical to real estate investing, requiring careful analysis, due diligence, and negotiation skills. You can identify lucrative investment opportunities and build a profitable real estate portfolio by sourcing potential opportunities, selecting properties that meet your investment criteria, conducting thorough inspections and financial analysis, and negotiating purchase agreements. Remember to stay informed about market trends, seek professional advice when needed, and continually refine your investment strategy to achieve long-term success in real estate investing. When the time comes, you'll be ready to scale your investments.

SCALING YOUR REAL ESTATE PORTFOLIO

Scaling and growing a real estate investment portfolio over time isn't as complex as it seems, and it gets easier with each investment. Eventually, you'll work from the investor mindset to explore options for diversifying investments, expand into new markets, partner with other investors, set ambitious goals, and leverage equity to finance additional investments.

When you're ready to scale, you'll want to consider your available strategies. These include:

- **Diversification**: Diversifying your real estate portfolio across different property types, markets, and investment strategies can help spread risk and maximize returns. Consider investing in residential, commercial, multifamily, and other property types and exploring alternative investment vehicles such as real estate investment trusts (REITs), syndications, and crowdfunding platforms.
- **Market expansion**: Explore opportunities to expand your real estate portfolio into new markets with strong growth potential, favorable economic conditions, and robust rental demand. Conduct thorough market research

to identify emerging markets, assess market fundamentals, and evaluate investment opportunities in different geographic regions.

- **Partnership opportunities**: Partnering with other investors, real estate professionals, or syndication groups can provide access to more significant deals, shared resources, and diversified expertise. Consider forming joint ventures, limited liability companies (LLCs), or real estate investment partnerships (REIPs) to pool capital, share risks, and pursue larger investment opportunities together.

- **Leveraging equity**: Use the equity in your existing real estate investments as leverage to finance additional acquisitions and expand your portfolio. Consider options such as cash-out refinancing, home equity lines of credit (HELOCs), or cross-collateralization to access equity and unlock capital for new investment opportunities. Be mindful of the risks and costs associated with leveraging equity and ensure that the benefits outweigh the potential drawbacks. Remember: good debt, not bad debt.

To confidently scale your real estate portfolio, stay informed about market trends, industry developments, and best practices in real estate investing through ongoing education, networking, and professional development. Attend seminars, workshops, webinars, and conferences, and seek mentorship from experienced investors or real estate professionals to enhance your knowledge and skills. Doing so is the best way to mitigate risks associated with portfolio growth.

Additionally, remain flexible and adaptable in your approach to portfolio scaling, as market conditions, economic trends, and regulatory changes may impact investment opportunities and strategies over time. Be willing to adjust your portfolio allocation, investment criteria, and risk tolerance to align with evolving market dynamics and achieve long-term success.

Scaling your real estate portfolio requires careful planning, strategic decision-making, and disciplined execution of your investment strategy. By diversifying investments, expanding into new markets, partnering with other investors, setting ambitious goals, and leveraging equity to finance additional investments, you can accelerate portfolio growth and achieve your financial objectives over time. Remember to prioritize risk management, adaptability, continuous learning, and patience in your real estate journey, and seek professional guidance when needed to maximize opportunities and mitigate risks along the way.

Ultimately, the key to successful real estate investing lies in adopting the investor mindset and a holistic approach that integrates passive and active strategies, diversifies across asset classes and geographical regions, and aligns with your long-term wealth-building objectives. By crafting a personalized wealth-building strategy with tangible assets, you can unlock the full potential of real estate as a vehicle for financial freedom and prosperity.

As someone who transitioned from financial struggle to financial freedom, achieving remarkable success in real estate, I can attest that real estate investments are a pathway to wealth accumulation. By adopting a proactive mindset and leveraging the power of real assets, you can also pave the way toward financial freedom and abundance. From capital protection and cashflow to tax advantages and inflation hedging, real estate investments provide a robust framework for building long-term wealth and financial security. Remember the words of Grant Cardone: 'Don't wait to buy real estate; buy real estate and wait.'

CHAPTER 8

NO ONE CAN PREDICT THE MARKET!

'BUY WHEN EVERYONE ELSE IS SELLING AND HOLD UNTIL EVERYONE ELSE IS BUYING. THAT'S NOT JUST A CATCHY SLOGAN. IT'S THE VERY ESSENCE OF SUCCESSFUL INVESTING.'

—J. PAUL GETTY

There's a misconception when it comes to the stock market, which is that with the right kind of information, you can learn to predict it. No one is a clairvoyant, so *no one can predict what will happen*. What you *can* do, however, is work with tools to increase your probability of winning and so make informed decisions. Let's have a look at what these tools might be, and how you can use them to help inform your strategy and hence improve your investment outcomes.

AI AND MACHINE LEARNING
IN MARKET ANALYSIS

Basically, AI helps you make informed decisions. It analyzes the market on your behalf, regardless of whether you're trading stocks, forex, crypto, or commodities, by identifying the market trends. It looks at whether it's trending up or down and provides signals indicating when to buy and when to sell. It does all this without the need for you to have the experience, time, and know-how. AI nowadays can do most of the heavy lifting for you without you having to lift a finger.

Markets are unpredictable. They're often volatile. And they can make us very fearful of what *might* happen. Thankfully, in this day and age, it's also possible to make use of technology to keep ourselves informed. Though a few years ago it would've seemed completely impossible to make decisions according to the information provided by computers and AI software, it's now completely different. AI and machine learning are changing the game!

But let's start with the basics, as you may not know what they are. Artificial Intelligence is the broader concept of machines being able to carry out tasks in a way that we consider 'smart'. Your mind most likely immediately jumped to ChatGPT— and it's true, it *is* a life-changing tool. But there's *so much more* to AI than ChatGPT. Within AI, we have the actual learning part, which is where the machine improves its knowledge over time by accessing more and more data. This is **machine learning**.

AI is now being used extensively in investing. For example, it's being used for **stock picking**. This is because new AI software is making it possible for investors to sort through all kinds of data incredibly efficiently, which then makes it easier for them to identify the stocks that meet their criteria. For example, you might want to use **stock screeners**, which are tools that allow you to filter different stocks based on all kinds of criteria that can include very specific (and necessary) technical data points, whether these are market capitalization, moving averages, accounting ratios, and so on—all types of data points that are available nowadays. In other words, machines are using these data points to suggest the most likely turn of events with certain stocks. It's similar to 95% interval tests in research —AI makes you more certain of the kind of investments you make, because it tests the specific data points to outline exactly which stocks might be best to invest in depending on the data points you're interested in analyzing.

Portfolio-building can also be automated through AI. For example, websites such as Wealthfront or Betterment that can make it easier for you to invest without having to know the entire market. As we saw in the previous chapter, this is often a point that makes a big difference in the kind of investor that you are—if you choose to be an active investor, you also need to be ready to keep track of all kinds of data points, which can be rather exhausting. So, this is where AI comes in. It can act as an advisor, but without the high advisor costs. It helps you outline your investment goals, takes note of your risk tolerance, considers time horizons, and much more—all with the goal of making your investments work effectively in the short *and* the long run. These automated portfolios essentially guide you through a questionnaire, then further guide you to the kind of model portfolio that would meet the criteria you have as an investor. This way, you can enter the investment market without needing to understand all of its ins and outs.

Trading and trade management is another area that can be aided by AI and machine learning. Remember our discussion on fear when trading? Well, new research has come out outlining how AI is changing the game because it's reducing the emotional aspect of trading. Simply explained, AI can help by being used to purchase a certain stock if it were to meet the criteria that a user is outlining. Then, it could also manage an exit strategy based on another set of criteria (e.g. using a stop). This way, there's much less stress when it comes to trading. In a way, it's creating a *hybrid* form of investment that incorporates the short-term nature of active investing, and the lower-risk aspect of passive investing.

You can also **optimize your portfolio** with AI. AI can be used to identify the kind of portfolio that works well for you based on your interests and criteria. Are you risk-hungry? How much money are you willing to invest? How much time are you willing to invest for? What are your goals? Nowadays, AI can compile all this information and give you a list of stocks to invest in that would match all this.

Finally, **data interpretation and predictions, as well as risk management**, are all alleviated by AI. As human beings, our capacity to compute data is limited. We can compute a lot of it, but not nearly as much as a computer can. On top of this, our ability to compute data is severely hindered by our feelings. When we get worried or scared, we stop thinking properly and we give into the fear that we might end up losing a lot. So, AI can step in here and make it easier for you to invest in a smart way. AI algorithms can allow a *prediction* about where a stock might go. It can interpret the market's data so as to give you more information on what to expect in the future. However, don't base all your investment decisions on AI. It's merely a *tool* that can make things easier for you, but it shouldn't *decide* for you. It's up to you to verify that the information provided by AI, and therefore the implications of this information, are true and accurate.

USING AI IN YOUR INVESTMENT ACTIVITIES

Let's consider how you can start to incorporate AI into your investment activities. First, you need to start by understanding your financial goals. No AI can help you if you don't know what you want to achieve, because its responsibility is to compute data. But how can it do this if it doesn't know what kind of data you'd like to compute?

Next, you need to choose the kind of investing method that works best for you. For example, will you want to work with a robo-advisor (e.g. an AI advisor) that does most of the work for you? Or, will you want to invest on your own? Of course, you can also work with a human advisor by using AI to analyze data, give them this information, and then leave it up to them to analyze whether the information is accurate.

Then, it's time to select an investment strategy. If you want to make your own investment decision, you should first determine the kind of strategy you're going to be using to make sure you know which kinds of stocks you want as part of your portfolio. Again, try to make use of AI here, such as by using robo-advisors.

Next up, look at the kind of tools you'll want to use while working on your investments. Do you want to use data analytics or AI tools? Portfolio managing tools? Consider looking into all the various options you have for your investments, then go from there.

Finally, once all this is set up, you're ready to start managing your portfolio. Remember, however, that AI isn't the be-all and end-all. You still have to double-check everything you do, because only following what AI tells you without questioning whether it's right can result in some serious problems. A small mistake made by AI, and not corrected by yourself, can truly lead you to lose a lot of money. Always do your due diligence!

In my opinion, relying solely on AI without verifying its suggestions can indeed have serious consequences. While artificial intelligence can be a powerful tool for decision-making and problem-solving, it's not flawless and can make errors.

Therefore, it's always crucial to verify the suggestions provided by AI through human judgment and critical thinking. Doing your due diligence ensures that you catch any errors or inconsistencies before they escalate into costly mistakes. Trusting but verifying is the key to harnessing the benefits of AI while mitigating its potential risks.

For example, let's consider algorithmic trading systems that use AI to analyze market data and execute trades automatically. While these systems can quickly process vast amounts of information and identify potential opportunities, they may also encounter unforeseen market conditions that could lead to errors. Failure to monitor and validate the system's decisions could result in significant financial losses.

Another scenario is the use of AI-powered robo-advisors for investment management. These platforms offer personalized investment strategies based on algorithms and historical data. However, overlooking important factors such as changing market trends or individual risk preferences could expose investors to unnecessary risks or missed opportunities.

In both cases, it's essential for users to remain vigilant and conduct their own research and analysis before making any decisions. By combining the strengths of AI with human judgment and due diligence, investors can better navigate the complexities of the financial markets and mitigate potential risks.

USING AI—EMOTIONLESS
TRADING SPECIALTY

At Winning Wallet, we use AI emotionless trading; we're incredibly passionate about AI. We *know* that it's the future. We know that to make the most out of it, and to emerge as winners, we have to use AI *right now* and ensure it becomes the new norm in the world of investment. But just as those who started out buying Bitcoin (which we'll discuss shortly) when it was initially launched have now made millions by buying them for a few hundred dollars, we see AI the same way: We need to use it *now* to make a lot more *later*. So, this is exactly what sets us apart.

When I first discovered the potential of utilizing AI for trading, it felt like uncovering a hidden treasure chest of opportunities. The idea that advanced technology could help me generate passive income and steadily grow my wealth was truly captivating. It wasn't just about making money; it was about embracing innovation and staying ahead in a fast-paced world. With the power of cutting-edge AI-driven trading, the possibilities seemed endless, and the journey towards financial empowerment became not just a goal but a thrilling adventure.

Interested in learning more about how we can help you achieve your goals? Reach out to us through @serge.dfouni

On that note, on to the next chapter.

CHAPTER 9

CRYPTO, BLOCKCHAIN, NFTs ... WHAT'S GOING ON?!

'IF YOU LIKE GOLD, THERE ARE MANY REASONS YOU SHOULD LIKE BITCOIN.'

—CAMERON WINKLEVOSS

We've talked mainly about the different kinds of 'traditional' investments that you can make. However, nowadays, traditional investment forms are no longer the only ones in the game. In fact, they're often very basic in comparison to all the other forms of investments that are possible! You might have learned about crypto, might know about blockchain, and may have also heard about NFTs. These are only a few examples of the kind of investments that you *can* make in this day and age. Unfortunately, too many people don't invest in them because they don't *understand* them, so they end up missing out entirely on great opportunities. So, let's have a look! This is truly the future—it's a *must* that you also know this is an option, and potentially start incorporating it into your investment strategy.

BITCOIN, CRYPTOCURRENCIES, BLOCKCHAIN—WHAT ARE THEY?

Once again, let's start with the basics. Cryptocurrency is a new form of money—one that isn't controlled by central banks, meaning that it's not regulated by interest rates or government agencies. Within this field, there's **Bitcoin**, which is the most well-known form of cryptocurrency. Bitcoin emerged in 2009 and introduced the world to not just a new currency, but also a groundbreaking technology called **blockchain**.

Let's first return to Bitcoin. This is a *digital asset* that was designed to work as a medium of exchange, using cryptography to secure transactions, control the creation of additional units, and verify the transfer of assets. In other words, it was created to use a specific language to control and verify the transitions taking place. It's solely virtual, *decentralized*, namely not controlled by any government or central bank as mentioned above. This is now one of its main selling points!

But what *really* makes Bitcoin (and other cryptocurrencies) work is blockchain technology. Imagine a ledger. Instead of it being kept somewhere in a bank, it's stored across a network of computers worldwide. Each block in a blockchain contains a number of transactions, and every time a new transaction occurs on the blockchain, a record of that transaction is added to every participant's ledger. So, the chain is transparent. It can't be changed or altered, and importantly, it's incredibly secure. In fact, it's increasingly being proposed as a way to address issues regarding corruption, because once a transaction is in the system, it can't be altered. Thus, money can't be stolen as easily, nor can it be sent from one politician to another without the others also being aware of it, as it's highly transparent.

Cryptocurrencies have since become an institution of their own. Bitcoin was just the starting point, and many other currencies have now been created—Ethereum, Ripple, Litecoin, Dogecoin, the list goes on. They all have different features and uses. This isn't just important to understand because it's the future. It is especially important for you as an *investor.*

Cryptocurrencies also entirely challenge the very way that we view money. Currencies no longer need to be confined to governments or central banks. They can now be created, exchanged, and managed by quite literally anyone with a computer and an internet connection! This means that new markets have arisen. New investment opportunities are now available, and we have new ways of thinking about how we invest and/or transfer our assets. Cryptocurrencies have forced banks, financial institutions, and even governments to rethink their roles in a world where financial intermediaries are no longer a *necessity,* so they've had significant impacts on traditional finance!

IS CRYPTO SAFE?

There are a few reasons why Crypto can be considered safe. For example, Bitcoin has a capped supply of 21 million coins, which is hard-coded into the protocol. This scarcity ensures that the value of Bitcoin is preserved, as it can't be diluted by creating more coins, unlike traditional currencies. So, you're able to safely invest without being worried about your currency being diluted—such as is the case in many countries due to high inflation! Besides this, Bitcoin also operates on a *decentralized network*, which means that no central authority can manipulate or control it. Therefore, you're able to feel much more secure in your investment! In fact, it's seen as *digital gold* because it's scarce and secure against inflation.

Bitcoin is often considered a reliable store of value in times of inflation due to its limited supply. Unlike traditional fiat currencies that can be printed endlessly by governments, Bitcoin has a predetermined maximum supply cap of 21 million coins. This scarcity helps protect it from the devaluation caused by inflation, as its value isn't subject to the whims of central banks or governments.

In a market affected by inflation, where the purchasing power of fiat currencies is eroded over time, Bitcoin's fixed supply can offer a hedge against such economic uncertainty. Investors often turn to Bitcoin as a way to safeguard their wealth and preserve its value in the face of rising inflation rates.

By holding an asset like Bitcoin that's immune to government manipulation and inflationary pressures, investors can feel more confident in the long-term stability of their investment portfolio. This unique characteristic of Bitcoin as a deflationary digital asset sets it apart from traditional monetary currencies and positions it as a potential resilience strategy in inflationary market conditions.

Likewise, the more people are on the network, the stronger the Bitcoin ecosystem becomes. The more demand there is, the higher the price will get. So, the earlier you start trading crypto, the better. For those who worry about its volatility, know this: As Bitcoin matures, more institutional investors and large corporations are showing interest in the asset. This increased demand from institutional players can lead to higher liquidity and greater price stability! Finally, it's also a great way to diversify your portfolio, which, as we've seen, is important when it comes to lowering your overall risk.

SHOULD YOU INVEST IN CRYPTOCURRENCIES?

Now, this is a complex and intricate question. On the one hand, crypto *is* a great option to make great returns. After all, Bitcoin has been shown to be extremely high in value, as you can see. On the other hand, it's *also* extremely volatile:

BITCOIN VALUE, DATED FROM 1ST JANUARY 2015 TO 31ST DECEMBER 2022.

Initial Capital	$100
2015	$232
2016	$477
2017	$6,988
2018	$14,800
2019	$54,077
2020	$256,869
2021	$1,200,070
2022	$1,775,367

It's therefore indeed a good investment, but it *does* entail significant risk. In fact, the volatility of cryptocurrency markets is legendary! Prices can soar and plummet by double-digit percentages within just a day. This can be due to various factors, whether that's market sentiment, regulatory news, technological advancements, or even just a tweet from a high-profile entrepreneur. So, needless to say, this might not be the right investment for a passive investor.

If you do want to invest in cryptocurrencies, you need to have a solid understanding of technology. You *also* need great market insights, and importantly, a **high appetite** for risk. For investors, the key is to understand the underlying value and potential of different cryptocurrencies. It *is* similar to traditional investing in that you need to assess risk, diversify your portfolio, and have a clear strategy. However, it does carry a lot more risk.

But it's the future! And, with the current inflation that we're witnessing, it's important that you invest your money because it's no longer safe to simply have it sitting in the banks. Banks all over the US and the UK are collapsing, so spreading your risk by investing in various kinds of fields, including crypto, can be a good way to alleviate this stress. You shouldn't limit yourself and your investments to only what you can understand—you should open yourself up to new options and new investment strategies, as long as you're ready to learn how to take care of them well and learn more about them.

My tip? Educate yourself. Make sure that you're as educated on the topic as you can be. Before you make any large investments, look at the information you have. *Do* use tools like AI and machine learning to help you establish whether this investment's a good idea, or whether you should hold off on it for a little bit more time.

WHAT ABOUT FOREX?

Foreign Exchange, most often known as Forex, is another form of investment you can make. This involves purchasing a currency and selling a different one simultaneously. Currencies are traded in pairs. For example, you might purchase Euros while selling US Dollars.

One of the great aspects of Forex is that the market is incredibly large and has a high level of liquidity. So, large amounts of money can be moved in and out of currencies, but with only minimal price movements. The market is also open 24 hours a day, five days a week. And yes, there is Crypto Forex! Some forex trading platforms have started to include cryptocurrencies as part of their currency pairs, and of course, crypto platforms allow you to exchange currencies as well.

INVESTING IN CRYPTO SAFELY

Crypto can be a fantastic investment—if you do it safely. A lot of money *can* be made, but a lot of money can also be lost! This is where you need to be especially careful, and where you have to watch out for a few key points. Educating yourself is the first step. Before you invest, you *must* understand what it actually is. You need to know what you're investing in *before* you do it without being fully educated. However, this can be a lot of new information to take on, and it can feel completely overwhelming if you don't know where to start. This is why we, at Winning Wallet, take care of all of this for you. We give you the opportunity to work with crypto without being completely on your own. We work *with* AI to give *you* the best opportunity to maximize your investment and make as much money as possible while minimizing your risk by using AI tools that help predict the market (to the best of its ability), and hence, lower your risk.

Likewise, you'll want to diversify your investments, as mentioned in a few other sections. Don't put all your eggs in one basket. Diversifying your portfolio across various cryptocurrencies can help mitigate risk. Remember, diversification is key in any form of investing! Again, this is something we help you with at Winning Wallet. Investing in stock indices, which we help you do, offers instant diversification, as it spreads risk across a *wide range of companies and sectors.* This reduces the impact of individual stock volatility and can lead to far more stable returns! Our goal is simple: We aim to make crypto more accessible for you by lowering the amount of risk you're facing. We use the newest tech to help you achieve this, so most of the risks associated with crypto become mitigated through AI.

In fact, advice regarding crypto often outlines that you should use reputable exchanges, because such platforms have better security measures and are more likely to provide assistance in case of any issues. This is something we also offer at Winning Wallet. We also help you with your long-term perspective, and help you have a clearer investment strategy. We help you prepare and protect yourself against volatility by using our tools. Specifically, Winning Wallet's automated trading system is designed to manage risk and execute trades based on predetermined parameters. This feature allows you to automate your trading strategy and minimize the risk of human error.

Do also make sure that you're understanding of the tax implications involved with your crypto investments. You don't want to make large profits without declaring them, because you may lose them all in fines!

Bitcoin ETF Approval—A Major Legislative Nod for Crypto!

For many intrigued by cryptocurrency, purchasing Bitcoin through an exchange remains a daunting, complex procedure. But complex technicalities like crypto wallets, endless Bitcoin addresses, and private keys add layers of confusion, deterring potential investors. Such challenges have made the concept of a Spot Bitcoin ETF (exchange-traded fund) increasingly attractive, offering a more straightforward way to gain Bitcoin exposure without the intricacies of direct ownership.

Well, the journey to this point hasn't been without its *hurdles*. After considerable delays and numerous rejections, January 2024 saw the US Securities and Exchange Commission (SEC) green-light several applications for Spot Bitcoin ETFs. On January 10, 2024, the SEC approved several Spot Bitcoin ETFs, allowing for trading shares in trusts holding BTC on regulated exchanges despite lingering issues. Among those now operating Spot Bitcoin ETFs in the US are leading financial giants, including BlackRock and Fidelity, paving easier investor access to Bitcoin.

Continuing down the path of more openness to cryptocurrencies, the SEC is expected to permit ETFs to include Ethereum as part of their holdings by May. According to a research report released on Tuesday by the bank, May 23 is the final deadline for the SEC to review ETF applications submitted by VanEck and Ark 21Shares.

So, What's the Difference between Spot ETFs and Future ETFs?

An ETF, or Exchange-Traded Fund, operates similarly to a stock in that it's traded publicly on a stock exchange. It *mirrors* the performance of an underlying asset or index, offering a diversified investment option compared to investing in a single company. This investment vehicle allows individuals to gain exposure to various assets, such as gold or oil, without directly owning them. As with traditional stocks, the value of an ETF tends to increase with the price of the underlying asset and decrease when the asset's price falls.

Well, the Spot Bitcoin ETF follows the same principles as any other ETF owning *actual* Bitcoin. It enables investors to purchase shares through their preferred brokerage, much like buying stocks in well-known companies like Apple or Tesla. The key difference is that Bitcoin ETFs specifically *track* the price of Bitcoin, aiming to mirror its market movements closely.

But before approving Spot Bitcoin ETFs, the SEC had approved two ETFs based on BTC futures in 2021. Bitcoin futures ETFs primarily invest in Bitcoin futures contracts (without owning Bitcoin *per se*), allowing investors to speculate on the future price of Bitcoin by agreeing to buy or sell it at a predetermined price on a specific date.

So, investing in a Bitcoin futures ETF means buying into a fund that holds these futures *contracts,* not Bitcoin *per se.* As such, this setup enables investors to trade the ETF similarly to traditional stocks, bypassing the need to directly engage in futures themselves, often resulting in lower fees than many crypto exchanges charge. Still, investing in a Bitcoin futures ETF doesn't involve buying Bitcoin at its current market price, leading some to question its authenticity as a form of crypto adoption.

EU Markets in Crypto-Assets (MiCA) Regulation

As one of the most exhaustive legislative crypto initiatives, the European Union, MiCA (Markets in Crypto Assets) legislation is set for a *gradual* rollout, bringing forth a set of crypto regulations that mandate new compliance requirements, implementing the 'travel rule' for crypto assets, and regulating digital asset service providers comprehensively.

As of December 30, 2023, the travel rule requires cryptocurrency companies to disclose information about both the sender and the recipient in a crypto asset transfer. Aimed at enhancing the traceability of cryptocurrencies, this rule serves as a tool against money laundering by ensuring transactions are transparent and accountable.

From now on, digital asset service providers face a mandate to secure authorization before operating. Their operations must adhere to established standards for governance, transparency, consumer protection, and risk management.

The takeaway? MiCA will likely weed out less credible players from the market, offering investors a more trustworthy pool of companies to engage with. Plus, the increased transparency would eventually make the crypto market more secure and reliable for investors by enhancing traceability and accountability, potentially reducing the risk associated with illicit activities. In this context, a refreshed focus on consumer protection means investors may benefit from clearer information, better protection against fraud, and standardized dispute resolution mechanisms.

Beyond the US and the EU—Other Regional Regulatory Developments

Any wise investor interested in cryptocurrency *should* become (at least a bit) familiar with the current developments around crypto legislation in other corners of the world. International bodies like the Financial Action Task Force (FATF), the International Monetary Fund (IMF), and the G20 are leading efforts to craft unified regulations for crypto-assets to address money laundering and digital asset sector risks. Key outcomes include the harmonized Anti-Money Laundering (AML) and Combating the Financing of Terrorism (CFT) standards to enhance the detection and prevention of illicit activities in digital assets.

Some reports indicate that China is moving forward with new AML rules for cryptocurrency in response to observations from the United Nations about the rise of crypto-related money laundering via underground traders within the country. Similarly, South Korea is enhancing its crypto regulatory framework to bolster its ambition of becoming a Web 3.0 development and adoption leader. Meanwhile, after a period of uncertainty, India appears ready to advance its regulatory framework for the cryptocurrency sector.

In the UK, efforts are underway to refine the regulatory landscape for crypto and stablecoins and sharpen its competitive edge against the EU's MiCA regulation. Prime Minister Rishi Sunak's administration is focused on updating the UK's legal and regulatory framework to strengthen its position as a center for financial innovation post-Brexit. Still, a critical issue for the UK will be balancing regulatory approaches to avoid dampening the cryptocurrency industry's enthusiasm, potentially deterring investment, which may not see a resolution in 2024.

Dubai, recognized for its dynamic regulatory approach with the Virtual Assets Regulatory Authority (VARA), offers a confidence-inspiring environment for both crypto-native and traditional financial firms. Its regulatory framework, part of the UAE's wider digital transformation strategy, makes the region a magnet for financial innovation. Hong Kong has positioned itself as the APAC leader by implementing regulations encouraging responsible crypto trading. The Hong Kong Monetary Authority (HKMA) is developing a comprehensive framework for stablecoin issuers, aiming for a 2024 rollout. The city's welcoming stance towards regulated retail crypto trading attracts major exchanges like ByBit, which is looking to use Hong Kong as a springboard for regional expansion.

Digital Dollars and Dimes ... Or the March Towards CDBCs

Central banks worldwide are exploring central bank digital currencies (CBDCs) to improve payment systems. CBDCs are the digital version of government-issued fiat money, not connected to commodities. They're produced by central banks, which formulate monetary policy, provide financial services to the government and commercial banks, and issue currency.

It turns out that *130* countries, representing 98% of global GDP, are investigating the use cases of CBDCs, a sharp increase from just thirty-five countries in 2020. The Bahamas and Nigeria were early adopters, introducing CBDCs to address specific national challenges. G7 countries like the UK and Japan are testing CBDC prototypes focusing on privacy and financial stability. China's digital yuan trial integrates over 200 use cases for 260 million people in CBDC adoption efforts. The European Central Bank, Australia, Thailand, and Russia are also advancing their digital currency projects.

Why all the fuss? Most of these initiatives seek to infuse the potential of the technology underlying cryptocurrencies but also to regulate the money supply more effectively, reduce transaction costs, and combat fraud. Besides, innovations in how digital assets are used and traded could attract investment in sectors that benefit from increased digital currency adoption.

The Countdown to Bitcoin's Halving

In early March 2024, according to NASDAQ, Bitcoin hit a new price record of US$73,237.70 up from $45,225.00 on January 1, 2024. With this surge, Bitcoin has now overtaken the precious metal silver in market capitalization. Contributing to this price increase was the anticipation of the '*halving*' event in April 2024, a mechanism that cuts in half the quantity of Bitcoin entering circulation through mining.

Bitcoin operates on a unique system where the reward for mining new blocks is cut in half roughly every four years, a process known as 'halving'. This is done to slow down the creation of new bitcoins, ensuring that the total supply of 21 million bitcoins isn't reached too quickly. Here's how it works: Miners use powerful computers to solve complex mathematical problems, and when they solve one, they add a new block of transactions to the Bitcoin blockchain. As a *reward* for their efforts, miners receive bitcoins. When Bitcoin was first launched in 2009, this reward was 50 bitcoins per block. And then, to ensure Bitcoin remains scarce and valuable, the reward for mining a block is halved every 210,000 blocks or roughly every four years.

So far, the rewards have been halved on *three* occasions: On November 28, 2012, the reward was halved to 25 bitcoins; on July 9, 2016, it was halved again to 12.5 bitcoins; on May 11, 2020, it dropped to 6.25 bitcoins. The next halving occurred on April 20, 2024, when the reward decreased to 3.125 bitcoins per block. It's a bit like a digital version of mining gold: Over time, it becomes harder and produces less new gold (or, in this case, bitcoins), making what's already mined more valuable.

Then, what should you expect? Bitcoin has risen dramatically in response to previous halvings. As a *domino* effect, the anticipation of reduced Bitcoin supply tends to lead to bullish market sentiment, which could be an opportunity for investors to capitalize on potential price surges. Even more, Bitcoin's halving may affect altcoins and market sentiment more generally in the cryptocurrency market. Anyway, investors should be quite attentive towards market movements and the potential effects of halving on other digital assets. As we know already by now, these dynamics can be unpredictable.

The bottom line is that no matter what kind of investment you're looking to make, your goal should be to make it *passively*. Investing in currencies can help you achieve this, likewise stocks in general. At Winning Wallet, our goal is to help you go one step further with your money. **We offer you one solution, but endless opportunities** by putting you in the driver's seat and giving you full control over your portfolio. Likewise, we help you stay ahead with data-driven decisions. With seamless integration with leading brokers like Binance,

Interactive Brokers, and Zerodha, Winning Wallet offers you access to comprehensive broker-generated reports and statements. This way, we help you make **well-informed decisions and fine-tune your trading strategies based on accurate insights and data.**

We also make sure to use **intelligent automation for maximum profits.** We use AI and machine learning to automate your trading strategies with *precision.* So, we make sure that you capitalize on profitable opportunities in the future landscape, while also minimizing human errors and emotions.

Finally, we secure your investments with advanced risk management, and we're always ready to support you through our dedicated customer support team.

CONCLUSION:
BE PREPARED FOR THE FUTURE

'THE BEST PREPARATION FOR TOMORROW
IS DOING YOUR BEST TODAY.'

—H. JACKSON BROWN, JR.

We're at the very beginning of a financial revolution. Crypto is growing increasingly important, and the future of finance is being rewritten before our very eyes. At Winning Wallet, we're passionate about bringing AI into your investment strategy in a way that makes *you* more money. We've seen how AI can process and analyze all kinds of datasets, and how it can give us insights and predictions that entirely redefine investment decision-making. So, embracing AI is no longer optional; it's essential for those who aspire to lead in the financial markets of tomorrow! We've also seen how the ride of decentralized finance, namely in crypto, is a promising new investment strategy considering the way that inflation is changing how we view money. Without central-ization, governments can't change the value of money, mak-ing Crypto a great option for those wanting to protect their assets and money from devaluation.

But embracing new technologies and investment paradigms isn't something we just *recommend*. To us, it's a call to action. At Winning Wallet, we encourage you to have a mindset of exploration and openness! We integrate AI into investment strategies, we *deeply* understand blockchain and digital assets, and therefore, we're dedicated to helping you align invest-ments with sustainable practices. There are no longer futuris-tic concepts—they're the reality, and now is the best possible time for you to make use of them before they become the new normal. They're not just another trend; they're what you need to get involved with *now* before it becomes too late. Stop missing out on the advantages that AI can provide—start making the most of them now!

If you've said 'I wish I'd invested in Bitcoin earlier' once in your life, this is your chance. It's your chance to make use of the newest technologies to boost your returns and minimize your risk. And for us, at Winning Wallet, it's *our* priority to make *you* happy with your returns. So, we have the tools and the platform that allow you to achieve just this.

'The biggest risk of all, is not taking one.'

Sincerely,
Serge El Dfouni

WORKS CITED

Byrne, R. (2006). *The secret.* Atria Books, New York.

Credit Suisse (2023). Credit Suisse Global Wealth Report 2023. https://www.credit-suisse.com/about-us/en/reports-research/global-wealth-report.html

Hill, N. (2007). *Think and grow rich: The landmark bestseller now revised and updated for the 21st century.* Penguin, London. (Original work published 1937.)

RisMedia (2024, May 3). Thoughts on leadership: PENAM— The architectural forces shaping you. https://www.rismedia.com/2024/05/03/thoughts-leadership-penam-architectural-forces-shaping-you/

UBS (2023). Projections of Global Household Wealth. https://www.ubs.com/global/en/family-office-uhnw/reports/global-wealth-report-2023.html

World Inequality Lab (2022). World Inequality Report 2022. https://wir2022.wid.world/www-site/uploads/2023/03/D_FINAL_WIL_RIM_RAPPORT_2303.pdf

ABOUT THE AUTHOR

Passionate about entrepreneurship, wealth creation, hospitality, real estate, and trading the financial markets, Serge El Dfouni thrives on identifying lucrative investment opportunities and leveraging them to create wealth and financial freedom. With a track record of success in both business and investing, he's built a diverse portfolio while achieving significant returns.

As a businessman, Serge launched and scaled multiple businesses, navigating the challenges of starting from scratch and building sustainable ventures. His expertise lies in creating innovative strategies, driving growth, and building high-performing teams. He's driven by a vision to make a positive impact and create opportunities for others. Today, he sits as a nine-figure shareholder and board member of a high-networth company.

In addition to his entrepreneurial pursuits, Serge is an avid investor in real estate, stocks, and cryptocurrencies. Through in-depth market research, analysis, and a disciplined approach, he's successfully capitalized on market trends and achieved impressive results. Serge believes in the power of strategic investing and continuously expanding knowledge in these dynamic markets.

EXTRAS/OFFER

So if you're interested in learning more about the AI Trading System the same way hedge funds and investment banks trade (which means your probability of making profits is extremely high) …

Reach out to me on @serge.dfouni to gain access to a FREE one-hour consultation where I or my team will show you everything you need to know.

It's unlike other trading techniques and skills …

You don't have to learn a new skill, have extensive experience, or put in a full-time effort …

Instead, you can rely on the accuracy of AI software that requires only **one hour a day**.

So. take the opportunities out there. Set up your risk management, and you're good to go.

It's that simple.

The best part is, you get to do this remotely from anywhere in the world.

All you need is a Wi-Fi connection and a laptop or phone.

If you're aiming to generate income and build your wealth, this is the way to do it.

If you're also interested in investing in real estate to produce positive cashflow from rental income while creating passive income, you can also reach out to me on Instagram at @signaturestaydubai or @serge.dfouni

NOTES